Author Jeannie Waters has p
Place at His Table. Intersperse
who's hungry for God's peace
a devotional to sink your teeth into. I'll keep extra copies of this wonderful
book on my shelf to share with those I love.

—Edie Melson
Award-Winning Author and
Director of the Blue Ridge Mountains
Christian Writers Conference

Find *A Place at His Table* and unwrap a gift from God's Word every day. You
will relish Jeannie Waters's reflections on the Scripture alongside heartwarming anecdotes from her life experiences. The practical applications of "Embracing the Gift" and "Sharing the Gift" make this more than a devotional
book, but a tool to help you savor the richness of the Christian life. If you
are craving pure spiritual milk (1 Peter 2:2), come to the table.

—Lisa Call, Missions Minister, Ingleside Baptist Church

Some days I need to be reminded of what I know to be true but sometimes
forget. That God loves me and promises to provide everything I need. That
He fills my life with good gifts and will never abandon me. Other days I just
need a hug. Jeannie Waters's new book, *A Place at His Table,* does all three.
A homespun mix of biblical truth and heart-hugging tenderness, *A Place*
makes me feel like I've run home to Mama to hear her tell me, "God loves
you and everything's going to be alright.

—Lori Hatcher, Author, *Refresh Your Hope: 60*
Devotions for Trusting God with All Your Heart

If you're looking for encouragement and practical ways to strengthen your
faith, look no further. Jeannie Waters's devotional, *A Place at His Table,* will
accomplish both. Drawing from personal experience and with the voice of
a wise teacher, the author shares real life stories you will easily relate to. Not
only that, but she also offers simple ideas that put your faith into action,
whether through thoughtful questions and self-reflection that result in your

own spiritual growth or with meaningful ways to serve others. This book will broaden your view of "table" in the most beautiful way, enabling you to see God where you might have previously missed Him.

—**Robin Dance**
Author, *For All Who Wander: Why Knowing*
God is Better than Knowing It All

A Place at His Table is my new favorite devotional.

Jeannie Waters's writing exudes her passion for encouraging others, and what better way than to point readers to what God has for us. Using a table theme, she invites us to have a seat and join her in partaking of the many treasures God places before us—if we but look! The author's voice is friendly, welcoming, and yet focused on the Lord who satisfies our every need.

With slices of humor and precious stories, I found it hard to not read ahead. But, just as a great meal is best enjoyed bite by savory (or sweet) bite, so too is A Place at His Table. Linger at Jeannie Waters's devotional table and do follow her suggestions under "Embracing the Gift" and "Sharing the Gift." You'll be blessed as much as you bless others. Grab a few extra copies for family and friends. Invite them to your table and surprise them with a gift of this devotional. It's for every season.

—**Lisa Loraine Baker**
Author, *Someplace to Be Somebody: God's Story*
in the Life of Marshall Brandon

Jeannie Waters invites us to take our place at God's table, tasting His goodness and nourishing our soul with the only One who can truly satisfy. While feasting around a table lavished with a buffet of gifts, the reader draws near to God through the relatable stories the author shares. Application strategies and call-to-action tips add a personal, practical touch too. What a marvelous way to feast with God! You'll enjoy each devotion so much, it'll be hard not to turn the page for a second helping!

—**Julie Lavender**
Author, *365 Ways to Love Your Child: Turning Little Moments*
into Lasting Memories and Children's Bible Stories for Bedtime

In *A Place at His Table,* southern author Jeannie Waters wraps us in a gentle hug and invites us to join her at God's table. Jeannie's devotion to Christ draws us to discover with her forty glorious gifts God gives His children every day. Gifts we too often forget or overlook in the heaviness and busyness of life. Jeannie leads us to slow down and linger over these beautiful treasures in God's Word, which she unwraps through her delightful stories.

—Jean Wilund,
Author, *Embracing Joy:*
A Transformational Bible Study of Habakkuk

With delightful creativity, Jeannie Waters invites us to dine at a variety of table settings, occasions, and life experiences. In these devotions, she draws parallels to God's timeless invitations to fellowship with Him regardless of time, place, or age.

In *A Place at His Table,* you will smile at Jeannie's warmth and personal accounts, but ultimately you will find God's invitations irresistible. This is a book you will want to read to remind you of God's creativity in faithfulness to us. It is the ultimate hostess gift to a friend.

—Marilyn Nutter, Co-author, *Destination Hope: A*
Travel Companion When Life Falls Apart

Jeannie Waters offers a loving invitation—engraved with your name—to dine at God's table. A place is reserved just for you. This table is like no other. It's full of satisfying abundance only God can provide. How comforting to know we belong there. For those of us whose table has recently felt bare or lonely, the author invites us to step right up to God's own table and receive His satisfying gifts every day. Reading this book, I was heartened by His joy and fullness. In Him is the satisfaction we've been craving. This book makes my heart feel like it's finally home again.

—Elizabeth Brickman, The Caring Advisor Podcast

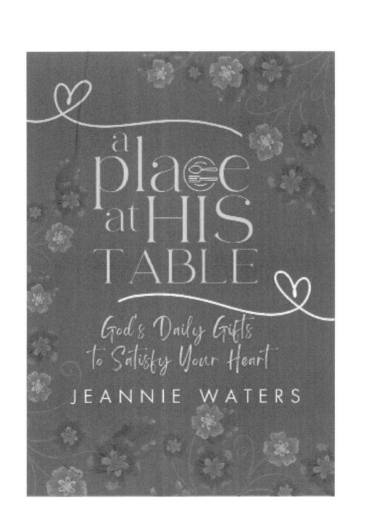

a
place
at HIS
TABLE

*God's Daily Gifts
to Satisfy Your Heart*

JEANNIE WATERS

a place at HIS TABLE

God's Daily Gifts to Satisfy Your Heart

JEANNIE WATERS

Bold Vision Books
PO Box 2011
Friendswood, TX 77549

ISBN 978-1-946708-96-0
Library of Congress Control Number 2023945546

All rights reserved.
Published by Bold Vision Books, PO Box 2011, Friendswood, Texas 77549
www.boldvisionbooks.com

Cover Design by Barefaced Creative Media - Amber Wiegand-Buckley
Interior design by WendyEL Creative.
Editing by Larry L. Leech II

Published in the United States of America.
1 2 3 4 5—27 26 25 24 23

DEDICATION

I dedicate this book to you, Ray, my knight in shining armor, my best friend, the love of my life. Sharing a table with you every day brings me joy.

Heavenly Father, Ray and I offer this book to You and pray You will be honored on every page and in every reader's heart.

You prepare a table before me … my cup overflows.

Psalm 23:5

Contents

AN INVITATION TO THE READER

Welcome, Dear Friend,

I'm glad you're here. Pull up a chair and let's talk about tables.

Whether a picnic table, an old painted table that became my desk or a sweet meal in my mama's country kitchen, tables have been a big part of my life. And in Jesus's life too.

Scripture paints word pictures of Jesus joining others around a table. He ate with His good friends Mary, Martha, and Lazarus, and with the scoundrel tax collector Zacchaeus. He dined with His disciples around a table before Judas betrayed Him in the garden.

In this devotional, we'll look at all kinds of tables, but the grandest one I want to share with you is God's. His table is filled with life-giving gifts to refresh and satisfy your heart.

God's table is a place of fellowship with Him. A place of community where we're never alone. A haven to take a deep breath and relax in. A place where it's okay to cry. It's also a joyful spot filled with acceptance, laughter, and unconditional love.

Early in the Old Testament, we read how God the Father instructed Moses to place a gold-covered table in the tabernacle—the table of the showbread. This table symbolized His presence with His people.

God's presence remains with His children today. He still provides daily gifts and precious promises for us on His table—like the manna He sprinkled on the desert floor for the Israelites. Exquisite treasures—blessings to meet our every need as well as truths designed to nourish our soul.

I'm thrilled to share these glorious truths with you. They make me stand on tiptoe each morning as I pray and anticipate the blessings God's placed on His table for me. For you. And for His name's sake. As David reminds us in Psalm 23:3, God's blessings are for our good, yes, but more importantly, they're for His name's sake.

Each day as you read this devotional, I encourage you to picture yourself unwrapping table gifts such as God's grace, compassion, and forgiveness. We'll even talk about a few gifts that, at first glance, don't look like gifts at all—but I promise they are. I hope you enjoy each devotion and the fun Table Tip associated with it.

Do you need comfort today? Find your place at His table.

How about wisdom? There's an extra helping for you.

Come hungry and allow God to fill you with servings of hope, joy, and refreshment. After we've feasted on God's blessings, we'll talk about how to share His gifts with others.

God invites you to pull up a chair to His table. He's set a place for you. Come as you are, in pajamas and slippers if you like—but come. "Oh, taste and see that the LORD is good" (Psalm 34:8).

I'll see you at the table,

—Jeannie

"You prepare a table before me."

Psalm 23:5

the gift of GOD'S ABUNDANCE

Our daughter, Tyler Marie, along with her future mother-in-law and me, faced choices—delectable ones. Chocolate hazelnut, almond amaretto, or white chocolate raspberry? Vanilla butter cake, Italian cream, or dulce de leche? We sampled each of the choices for Tyler Marie's wedding cake.

Deborah, our master cake designer, set the table with glass plates, silver forks, and a trayful of cake slices. She described the flavors with mouth-watering detail while we drooled over her wedding cake portfolio.

The slices of scrumptious goodness seemed to originate in heaven instead of a baker's oven. As our taste buds saluted her work, Deborah listened to our soft *hums* of delight over each flavor. When we couldn't choose, she rescued us. "You could select a different type of cake for each of the four layers if you like."

"Yes!" the three of us said through icing-laced lips.

Tyler Marie made her choices. "Two layers of chocolate hazelnut and one layer each of almond amaretto and white chocolate raspberry please. And I'd like buttercream frosting with the fondant lace in this picture."

Happy bride, happy baker.

Deborah's exquisite design helped make Tyler Marie's wedding dreams come true. Our Father God is the Master Designer. He surpasses our dreams with the greatness of His presence, power, and gifts. So many gifts from the very beginning.

God spoke the world into existence and designed blessings from His Father's heart and unlimited riches. He's lavished the world—and us—with more than we could ever imagine (1 Corinthians 2:9). He "richly provides us with everything to enjoy" (1 Timothy 6:17). Spiritual blessings that fill us with the delight of a bride on her wedding day.

The abundant life God promises us reminds me of mountain waterfalls, spilling over with joy and purpose. The goodness of our Creator pouring out rain on corn and wheat fields and creating puffs of cotton on woody stems. Stretching out majestic mountains and vast oceans that testify to His awe-inspiring creation power. He also provides us with gracious supplies of wisdom, comfort, peace, mercy, and grace.

Best of all, our Father gifts us with eternal life in heaven and an abundant life with Him for all who will believe in Christ (John 10:10). In Him, we receive the undeserved gift of a close personal bond, not like a distant relationship with third cousins once removed who we see only at family reunions. With them, conversation ends after "Good to see you" and "How's Aunt Susie?" Our heavenly Father knows us, and we learn more about Him each time we read His Word and enjoy conversation in prayer.

God sets an exquisite table for His children filled with heavenly portions of blessings. He includes frosting-on-the-top gifts, such as prayer, rest, comfort, and opportunities to serve others. He adds friendship, a child's laughter, the fragrance of a rose, multi-colored sunsets, the freshness of spring rain, a fire on a cool evening—all rich blessings for our good that we might reflect His glory.

David said to God, "You prepare a table before me in the presence of my enemies" (Psalm 23:5). The shepherd who became king

TABLE TIP

CHARCUTERIE BOARD ABUNDANCE

Charcuterie platters offer variety in color and taste. Make it as simple or elaborate as you'd like for a meal, snack, or appetizer. Use a tray, plate, or cutting board. Or even butcher paper. Green or red grapes paired with cheese and crackers create a simple but attractive and delicious treat.

rejoiced that God didn't just prepare a table for him, but one in the presence of his enemies. David knew his God to be gracious. "I shall not want," he said (v. 1). The Lord is his Shepherd—his gracious Shepherd. And his delight because David trusted in Him.

Our gracious Lord prepares a table for us too. A table more abundant "than all that we ask or think, according to the power at work within us" (Ephesians 3:20). He's willing and able. We might fail to notice God's blessings though if we're preoccupied with what we *don't* have.

On our Father's table, we find an abundance of His daily gifts, tailor-made not only to meet our needs, but also to satisfy our hearts. I'm thankful we don't have to choose a limited number of His blessings like the choices we faced with the glorious cake and frosting for Tyler Marie's wedding. We can enjoy each one.

*Now to him who is able to do far more abundantly than
all that we ask or think, according to the power
at work within us.*

Ephesians 3:20

LET'S PRAY

*Father, You give perfect gifts. In addition to supplying all I
need, You bless me with extra gifts. Thank You for this morning's sunrise and hot coffee. Thank You for prayer and opportunities to serve You. Show me how to honor You and serve
others each day with Your abundant blessings. Amen.*

EMBRACING THE GIFT

Draw three columns on a sheet of paper. In one column, list life-sustaining gifts we often forget to thank God for, such as rain, air, and sunshine. In the second column, list spiritual blessings He's poured out for you, such as peace, forgiveness, and answers to prayer. In the third column, list God's frosting-on-the-top gifts you enjoy like white lace, yellow tulips, and delicious wedding cake. Spend some time in prayer to thank Him for each gift.

SHARING THE GIFT

Select an inexpensive gift for someone you know. Write on a card, "I'm grateful for God's abundant gifts in my life. You are one of those gifts, so I want to bless you with this small present as a reminder." Perhaps a fun coffee mug, a small bouquet of flowers, or gourmet cupcakes will remind them of the Father's abundant blessings—including friendship.

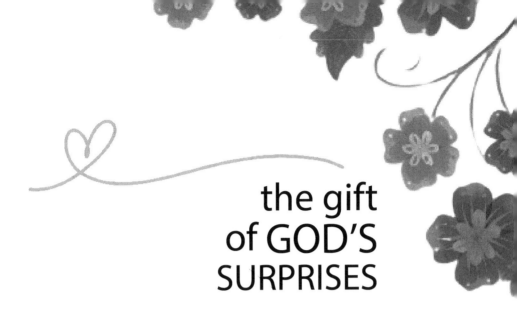

the gift
of GOD'S
SURPRISES

A special guest accepted my lunch-in-the-park invitation. Once I announced the picnic plans on a school holiday, our young son and daughter peppered me with questions. "Who's the special guest for the picnic, Mom? When are we leaving? Can we play on the playground when we get to the park?"

"It's a secret, but you'll see when we get there. We're leaving soon, and yes, you may play on the playground."

As soon as we arrived at our favorite park, Matt and Tyler Marie jumped out of the car and dashed toward the playground equipment. I covered the table with a tablecloth and created a centerpiece with camellia blossoms and the jelly jar I'd packed. Tyler Marie joined me to unpack a lunch of sandwiches, chips, fruit salad, and oatmeal cookies. Matthew sprinted back to the table to show me a blue jay feather he'd found.

For what seemed like the one-hundredth time, the children asked about the guest. "Who's coming, Mom? Who's the special guest?"

I responded with a smile. "He's driving up now."

Emerging from the car was none other than Ray, my husband, their daddy—our surprise guest. The children ran into his open arms and smothered him with hugs and kisses. When the 'welcome ceremony' ended, I asked, "Is anybody hungry?"

After Ray prayed, we gathered around the table and filled our plates. He smiled again when he saw *his* surprise—a slice of homemade pound cake, his favorite dessert.

While he ate his cake, the children begged him to play. "Daddy, are you finished? Will you come push me on the swings?"

I repacked the picnic basket and walked across the park to join them. Tyler Marie's laughter mixed with a plea. "Daddy, push me higher so my toes touch the sky." After the children stopped swinging and raced to the monkey bars, Ray climbed with them—up to the top.

Before he left to return to work, he dusted off his shoes and hugged me. "Thanks, Honey. It's been a hectic morning. I needed family time—and the pound cake—but surprising the kids was the best. I loved seeing their faces when I drove up." After a group hug, Ray got in his car and returned to the office.

Within His sovereign plans, our heavenly Father has surprises waiting for us as well. Both here on earth and in heaven. In His Word, He's told us all we need to know to live in the center of His will, but there's much He still hasn't told us. "The secret things belong to the LORD our God, but the things that are revealed belong to us and to our children forever, that we may do all the words of this law" (Deuteronomy 29:29).

Glorious surprises wait for us in heaven, and some of His promises remain mysterious to us today. "For now, we see in a mirror dimly, but then face to face. Now I know in part; then I shall know fully, even as I have been fully known" (1 Corinthians 13:12).

We can trust God for what we don't understand, obey what He's clearly revealed in the Bible and look with excitement toward the joys ahead—pleasures forever.

He also designs surprise gifts on the paths of our earthly life. My tea olive shrub blooms at unexpected times. Its sweet fragrance

TABLE TIP

PICNIC SURPRISE FUN

Create a new tradition with picnics. Select a special location or dessert for each season. Keep one food a secret to surprise friends or family. In your picnic basket or box, place a container to hold a card for each picnic. Record the date, menu, location, and special memories from each occasion on a card. Read the cards the following year and vote on the favorite picnic.

prompts me to breathe deeply and relax. Recently, when I'd craved pears, a friend brought me a bagful of delicious fruit from her tree. FaceTime calls from children and impromptu visits by friends brighten my day and remind me of my heavenly Father, who loves to surprise His children.

The secret things belong to the LORD our God, but the things that are revealed belong to us and to our children forever, that we may do all the words of this law.

Deuteronomy 29:29

LET'S PRAY

You're such a good Father, God, and every day with You is an adventure. You provide all I need and even design surprise gifts which delight me. Remind me to thank You for the sweet surprises You tuck into each day and the amazing ones that await me in heaven. In Jesus's name, I pray. Amen.

EMBRACING THE GIFT

Reflect on the unexpected joys you discovered last week. Did you admire a stunning sunset or catch a glimpse of a rainbow? Perhaps you heard a child's giggle or the clear notes of a songbird. Did a friend's call or an opportunity to help someone bring joy? Write a list of each unexpected joy you remember and add an exclamation mark as you thank God for surprise gifts.

SHARING THE GIFT

Share an unexpected blessing with a friend or stranger. You may not get to witness their smile and gratitude, but God will. Consider paying for the meal of the driver behind you in a restaurant drive-through or drop off ingredients and a simple recipe to a busy mom—or cook the meal for her. A sincere thanks to a store clerk can soften the sting of complaints by other customers. When you surprise another person, you can add joy to their heart—and yours—and delight your Father in heaven.

the gift
of GOD'S
UNCONDITIONAL
LOVE

Have you ever eaten pink grits? I have.

Every Valentine's Day of my southern childhood, Mama made a special breakfast. She tinted our grits pink and covered heart-shaped biscuits with strawberry jam. Glasses of red punch and heart-speckled napkins added pizazz to the festive meal. Beside our plates, Mama placed small presents, candy treats, and red hearts she'd pasted onto white paper doilies.

With great anticipation, I'd rush my brothers to the table. "Hurry up! It's Valentine's Day. Come look at the table."

Carson and Ed would run to the table with their eyes wide. "Chocolate candy!" one of them would say. "Can we open our gifts now?" the other would ask.

Normally, Mama didn't allow candy at her table, but on Valentine's Day she delighted us with sweet treats and a memorable breakfast. Mama loved to bless us with surprises even though my two brothers and I didn't always run to the table with cheerful dispositions or obey her rules perfectly. She still sent us off to school with smiles, happy tummies, and the best gift of all—her unconditional love.

In a much greater way, God showed His unconditional love at the cross. He gave the best gift of all. In an unprecedented act of love, while we were still sinners and enemies of God, He offered us His innocent Son. Jesus Christ willingly bore our sins on the cross and paid the penalty so we don't have to (Romans 5:8). His endless love for us surpasses even the greatest parents' love. Even Mama's.

Some earthly moms and dads remain distant and fail to demonstrate love, but believers are never ignored, rejected, or estranged from our Father in heaven. The psalmist described God this way: "But you, O Lord, are a God merciful and gracious, slow to anger and abounding in steadfast love and faithfulness" (Psalm 86:15).

God's love never fails. It's constant and active. He answers prayer, shows patience, and even paves the way back to full fellowship with Him by forgiving us when we confess our sin (1 John 1:9).

In Luke 15, Jesus told a parable about a father who showered unconditional love onto his rebellious son. This younger son demanded his inheritance early and left home. Then he "squandered his property in reckless living" (v. 13).

Searing hunger and destitution drove the prodigal son to crave even the slop he fed his master's pigs. Utterly broken, he returned home to ask his father if he could work as a slave. Forgiveness was too much to even imagine.

The prodigal son's father saw him while he was a long way off and, throwing off all dignity, ran to greet him. He hugged and kissed his son and planned a celebration of his return with lavish gifts and an extravagant 'welcome home' meal. He rejoiced over his rebellious son's homecoming, and he responded with forgiveness and unconditional love. Just as our heavenly Father does. The more we learn about Him, the more we'll understand the depth of His love.

Mama only served pink grits and chocolate treats for breakfast once a year, but God arranges expressions of love on His table 365

TABLE TIP

AN APPLE A DAY

Keep me as the apple of your eye; hide me in the
shadow of your wings.

Psalm 17:8

Display this verse on your table along with a bowl of apples as a reminder of God's unconditional love. His children are precious to Him and He watches over us. For one week, incorporate apples into your meal plan. Just for fun, include as many choices as you can from the rhyme below.

Apple juice, apple salad,
apple cobbler, pie, and crisp,

Apple slices, apple fritters,
apple tarts, apple bisque.

days a year. Our heavenly Father's steadfast love rises with the sun and shines through the night with the stars and moon every day of our lives—and forever.

God shows his love for us in that while we were still sinners,
Christ died for us.

Romans 5:8

LET'S PRAY

Father God, Your love astounds me. Thank you for loving me unconditionally. I could never deserve such faithful love. Help me savor the indescribable expressions of Your love and share them with others. In the name of Jesus who loves us, I pray. Amen.

EMBRACING THE GIFT

This week, look for God's love messages as you read the Bible. Note the verses that reveal how much God has shown His great love for us. For you. Write the verses out and treasure them like a valentine from the Lord that says, "I love you." Notice examples of His love in the world around us. Today, maybe you noticed beautiful music, rain-promising clouds, or the shade under a giant tree. Did you enjoy a conversation with a friend?

SHARING THE GIFT

Sprinkle expressions of God's love on your daily path as you meet others. His unconditional love is far too precious a gift to keep to ourselves. "Beloved, let us love one another, for love is from God, and whoever loves has been born of God and knows God" (1 John 4:7).

Start a 'Favorites' collection in a notebook or phone app. List people you want to bless—a neighbor, a friend, a coworker, or family member. As you notice their favorite songs, flowers, colors, candy, or hobbies, make a note. For special occasions or when a person on your list needs a lift, share a small gift or even a picture with a note that says, "When I saw this, I thought of you." Include a Bible verse and thank God for the privilege of sharing His unconditional love.

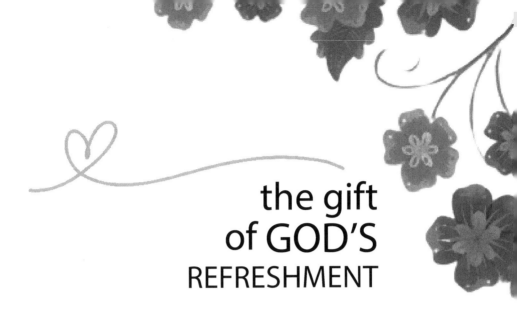

the gift
of GOD'S
REFRESHMENT

Red-faced and sweaty from the afternoon summer sun, my ten-year-old brother, Ed, ran like the deer we'd spotted across the river mid-morning. "I'll beat you to the spring," he called.

I sprinted behind him and responded with big-sister confidence. "Oh no, you won't." We raced from our sunny, rock-skipping post beside Amicalola Creek to the shade of the moss-covered hillside, our favorite spot at our grandparents' mountain cabin.

Ed reached the spring first. "Beat ya." He gulped the icy water pouring from the pipe Granddaddy had hammered into a natural spring between large rocks. I leaned over, my hands on my knees, to catch my breath. After Ed drank his fill, he swiped his arm across his mouth, leaving streaks of dirt on his suntanned face. "Your turn."

I cupped my hands and drank water until its coolness revived me. We splashed the water on our faces and rubbed it over our arms. Re-vitalized, we ran off to play again until mid-afternoon when we went inside, plopped into the red vinyl chairs at the Formica-topped table, and waited for a snack.

Our grandmother would often serve us warm banana nut bread slathered with butter. I remember chasing the last few crumbs across the blue and white china plates with my fork before we'd push open the screen door and resume our play. The snack filled our tummies, but the spring water refreshed us.

I often remember Granddaddy's spring when I read David's words in Psalm 42:1-2. "As a deer pants for flowing streams, so pants my soul for you, O God. My soul thirsts for God, for the living God." David didn't race his brother. He ran for his life. He was soul-weary from King Saul's relentless attempt to kill him, and he needed the energizing spring of God's mercy and comfort.

Like me, maybe you've experienced difficult seasons that parched your soul. In those times, we can pray, and trust God as David did. Our heavenly Father knew our hearts would grow weary and discouraged, and He knew we'd experience the fatigue of work and life's challenges. He offers living water—water far more revitalizing than any mountain spring.

Jesus told the Samaritan woman anyone who drinks physical water will thirst again, then He promised, "but whoever drinks of the water that I will give him will never be thirsty again. The water that I will give him will become in him a spring of water welling up to eternal life" (John 4:14). Convinced of her need, the woman at the well responded in faith. "Sir, give me this water, so that I will not be thirsty" (v. 15).

Like the Samaritan woman, we who believe on the Lord Jesus Christ (Acts 16:31) hold assurance of His Spirit in us—a life-giving spring, for life now and throughout eternity. We can enjoy His presence throughout each day.

After demanding work or emotional trauma, we can run to Him and embrace the promises of His Word to meet our every need. After a wrestling match with worry or fear, or a skirmish with false guilt or pride, His presence assures us of His strength to continue the fight (Psalm 73:26). We can depend on His reassurance when we're bruised by disappointment or an unkind comment.

Sometimes our heavenly Father designs a gift of refreshment especially for us. Cool breezes on hot days extend the time I spend on

TABLE TIP

REFRESHING TREATS

Make a glass of iced coffee.

Add lemon or lime slices or berries to iced tea.

Drop slices of cucumbers or strawberries into water for a refreshing drink.

Place carrot and cucumber sticks in a jar of water and refrigerate for a crunchy snack.

Make a smoothie with frozen fruit and plain Greek yogurt. Add a handful of spinach for nutritious value.

my deck and help me take a deep breath. When I'm tired, a cold glass of water sometimes sparks memories of the mountain spring and prompts me to smile and rest.

The presence of God and the promises in His Word offer daily gifts to revive our souls. Does your heart need a refill of His living water?

Our heavenly Father offers greater refreshment than an ice cold pitcher of spring water on a hot summer day. Find a quiet place to meet with Him, drink deep of His living waters, and unwrap His gift today.

As a deer pants for flowing streams,
so pants my soul for you, O God.
My soul thirsts for God, for the living God.

Psalm 42:1-2

LET'S PRAY

Heavenly Father, when life leaves me tired and thirsty, help me turn to You and the springs of living water you provide. Renew my heart today with Your presence. Help me speak words of life and lighten the loads of people on my path by offering acts of service—even if it's only a cup of cool water. Amen.

EMBRACING THE GIFT

Do you feel weary, discouraged, and exhausted? Grab a glass of cold water or lemonade and your Bible. Meditate on Psalm 42. Allow God's presence and promises to renew your heart today.

SHARING THE GIFT

God sometimes breathes new life into our hearts through the encouragement of fellow believers. The apostle Paul included examples in his letters (Philemon 1:7, 20; 2 Corinthians 7:13). Write a note to a weary servant of the Lord you know or offer a helping hand to encourage them. Maybe you know a struggling single mother or health-impaired senior. Could you help with a home repair, make a trip to the grocery store, or a share a chat over coffee? Jesus commended believers who would offer even a cup of water to a person in need (Matthew 10:42). Let's share the refreshment He gives to us with someone this week.

the gift
of WORDS

As a high school student, I shared the events of my day and my opinions with my family around the dinner table—except for critical comments about classmates and teachers because Daddy prohibited it.

He would stop me mid-sentence with a stern reminder. "Nope. Keep the gossip and negative thoughts to yourself. You never know what's going on in someone else's life."

I silently questioned his judgment. Gossip? Surely my comments didn't qualify as gossip. I only shared them with my family, and besides, I told the truth as I saw it. How could my critical comments hurt anyone?

One night after Daddy's correction, I recalled the words we'd said on our elementary school playground after name-calling matches. "Sticks and stones may break my bones, but words will never hurt me." But they can. Daddy taught me this. And so does Scripture.

"Let no corrupting talk come out of your mouths, but only such as is good for building up, as fits the occasion, that it may give grace to those who hear" (Ephesians 4:29). Daddy was right. Words matter. I want mine to build others up, not tear them down.

Words are God's gifts to use for His purposes. He used them to create the world and declare of Jesus, "This is my Son, my Chosen One; listen to him!" (Luke 9:35). He tells us to use words to offer comfort, godly wisdom, and the gospel of salvation. To "rejoice with those who rejoice, weep with those who weep" (Romans 12:15). To speak His gracious and powerful Truth so we can add nourishment and delight to those around us.

My friend June welcomes guests and members to our Sunday morning class with kindhearted words. She adds comfort, encouragement, and godly wisdom to warm conversation and leaves others with a smile.

With God's gift of words, we can praise Him in song, talk with Him in prayer, and read the sacred Scriptures—the most precious and powerful of all words. The words of life (John 6:63).

Scripture influences our speech. The Bible writer James compared the strength of the tongue to a rudder's ability to turn a ship and a small fire's capacity to ignite a forest (James 3:4-6). The searing words we say can burn long-lasting scars into others' hearts. We may say, "I take that back" or "I'm sorry," but reclaiming words is like trying to retrieve helium balloons that slip from our grasp and float into the clouds. We can't get them back.

Daddy helped me see that sometimes my comments burned and scorched others' hearts or reputations. He taught me to control my tongue and steer it toward words that are "like apples of gold in a setting of silver" (Proverbs 25:11). Words are God's gifts to use for His purposes.

King Solomon used a phenomenon of nature to describe the value of grace-filled or pleasant words. "Gracious words are like a honeycomb, sweetness to the soul and health to the body" (Proverbs 16:24). When we fill our speech with scriptural truth, God stores our words in the hearts and minds of listeners like honeybees store their precious golden liquid in the honeycomb.

TABLE TIP

SWEET AS HONEY

Gracious words are like a honeycomb,
sweetness to the soul and health to the body.

Proverbs 16:24

Place a jar of honey on the table. Fold an 8.5-inch x 11-inch piece of stiff paper into thirds to make a table tent. Unfold and write Proverbs 16:24 on the paper. Decorate it if you'd like. Tape the unfolded sides together to secure the triangular table tent. Place the table tent beside the honey as a reminder to speak gracious words.

Daddy could have placed a jar of honey on the dinner table to remind us to treasure God's gifts of words. But then again, we didn't need one. Daddy was our reminder. He spoke gracious words and taught us to do the same.

Let no corrupting talk come out of your mouths, but only such
as is good for building up, as fits the occasion, that it may give
grace to those who hear.

Ephesians 4:29

LET'S PRAY

Heavenly Father, I'm grateful for Your Word and the new life in Christ You offer through it. I want my words to honor You and reflect Truth. Give me wisdom to know when to speak as I look to You in conversation. Fill my heart with words that edify others and taste like honey. Amen.

EMBRACING THE GIFT

When my friend Jenny and I eat lunch together or take a day trip, she prays the words of Psalm 19:14 for us. "Let the words of my mouth and the meditation of my heart be acceptable in your sight, O LORD, my rock and my redeemer." The verse reminds us to honor God with our words as we talk and refrain from conversation He warns against in His Word. Try this helpful practice.

SHARING THE GIFT

As you read the Bible today, ask God to give you the words someone needs this week. Maybe you'll call a family member who needs to hear about God's faithfulness or text a friend who needs reassurance they can take their burdens to the Lord like you've done for them in prayer. A cashier or a neighbor may need a smile and a reminder of God's love. Words matter. They're a gift. Be a lavish gift giver.

the gift
of HUMILITY

The first time I joined Ray's extended family for a meal, my mother-in-law's dinner protocol shocked me. Why did Carolyn give the men priority to fill their plates and claim seats at the table before us?

How rude.

In my family, it's ladies first.

Harboring a critical spirit, I stood in the kitchen at the back of the line with my arms folded and my stomach growling. The sound of men's laughter roared from the dining room.

While they ate turkey and dressing and sweet potato soufflé, we ladies filled our plates. My sweet mother-in-law, who'd prepared the meal, insisted her daughters-in-law and grandchildren go ahead of her.

Determined to set things right, I put my hand on Carolyn's shoulder. "Go ahead and fix your plate and sit. You've worked so hard to cook all this food."

She looked stunned. "No, I'm fine. You fix *your* plate."

I looked to my new sisters-in-law for support. They shrugged.

Like a five-star-restaurant-trained server, Carolyn refilled glasses with sweet tea until the last serving of blackberry cobbler was spooned into a bowl. Puzzled, I watched.

Why did she choose to eat last after standing on her feet for days to prepare a *Southern Living Magazine*-worthy feast for thirty people? Why did she encourage the men to go first?

After dinner, I overheard a conversation between two sisters-in-law.

"Carolyn has a servant's heart, doesn't she?" one said. "She's so humble. She always thinks of others before herself and genuinely enjoys serving us."

"Yes, she does," the other said. "I heard her say she likes for the men to go first and sit together because it's the only time all year her sons see each other. She loves to refill their glasses and listen to them reminisce about old times."

My mother-in-law chose to serve and eat last.

Rude?

Not at all.

Perhaps her actions nourished her resolve to honor others before herself. Unlike me, she didn't desire her rightful place at the dining table. The humble lady we loved followed Jesus's example.

The Son of God surrendered His rightful place in heaven and came to earth in human flesh (Philippians 2:5-7). He slept in an animal feeding trough in Bethlehem and rode a donkey into Jerusalem. He rested not in a palace, but in the homes of others or under the stars.

Jesus served in practical ways with the humility of a servant. He fed crowds much larger than those at my mother-in-law's house (Luke 9:10-17) and washed the dusty feet of His disciples (John 13:1-16). After they argued about which of them was the greatest, Jesus said, "If anyone would be first, he must be last of all and servant of all" (Mark 9:35).

While I watched my mother-in-law and pondered the character of Christ, I recognized myself as a servant-in-training eating a large slice of humble pie. Although I'd longed to be more like Jesus, I'd missed a key trait—humility.

TABLE TIP

CAROLYN'S EASY FRUIT COBBLER

My dear, humble mother-in-law picked her own peaches or blackberries to make this cobbler.

Preheat the oven to 350 degrees.

Melt 1 stick of butter and pour it into a baking pan or dish.

Whisk together to mix: ¾ cup of self-rising flour, ¾ cup of milk, and 1 cup of sugar.

Add the flour mixture to the pan, but do not stir in with the butter.

Simmer ½ cup of sugar mixed with ¾ cup of water until the sugar dissolves.

Stir 1½ cups of fruit into the sugar-water mix. Simmer for 1-2 minutes.

Pour the fruit mix onto the top of the flour mixture. Do not stir.

Bake 35-45 minutes.

Serve warm.

The prophet Micah asked his people, "What does the Lord require of you but to do justice, and to love kindness, and to walk humbly with your God?" (6:8). My mother-in-law met all three requirements and set an example for me.

Like Carolyn, humble people esteem others above themselves rather than holding attitudes of pride and arrogance. An honest realization of the supremacy of God and His love for us make us eager to walk humbly with Him.

When we long to be more Christlike and remember the precious nature of relationships, we are more likely to pick up the gift of humility and the service opportunities God places on the table. Humility helps us avoid pride, selfishness, and a critical spirit—all displeasing to God and serious hindrances to relationships.

Like my mother-in-law who followed her Lord, we honor God and bless others when we serve with a humble spirit. This servant-in-training learned a lot.

What does the LORD require of you
but to do justice, and to love kindness,
and to walk humbly with your God?

Micah 6:8

LET'S PRAY

Dear God, I want to serve You with a humble heart. Continue to teach me and help me put the needs of others before mine. Lead me to follow the example of Jesus, who served people when He walked on earth. In His name I pray. Amen.

EMBRACING THE GIFT

Consider Bible characters who exemplified humility. Joseph, for instance. His brothers threw him in a pit and sold him as a slave. Years later in Egypt when they recognized him, they trembled in fright at his power. Joseph spoke to them with humility before God. "And now do not be distressed or angry with yourselves because you sold me here, for God sent me before you to preserve life" (Genesis 45:5). Ask God to give you a humble heart like Joseph's and opportunities to serve others, even those who may have wronged you.

SHARING THE GIFT

Watch for humble servants in your family and church and among friends. Thank them for the Christlike characteristics you notice in their lives. As you walk with God this week, you may allow others to talk more, pull into the best parking space, or go first through a serving line. The gift of humility helps us serve others.

the gift
of PRAYER

We couldn't read a single word on the menu. On the first night in Germany, our family of four hoped for English translations while we scanned the entrées. Our German vocabulary consisted of *yes, no, thank you,* and *Where's the restroom?*

From the server's voice inflections, we understood she was asking a question. We smiled and nodded as typical English-only speakers. She left our table and returned with four glasses of water. Success for the American tourists.

The server stood poised with pen in hand. Finally recognizing an entrée, I said, "*Wiener Schnitzel.*" Our daughter, Tyler Marie, echoed, "*Wiener Schnitzel.*"

"I'll have *Wiener Schnitzel,*" Ray said in his best German.

After a laugh, guess what our son ordered.

Choosing pastries at the German bakery required different expertise. Proud of my ability to order in another language, I pointed to a delicacy in the glass case, held up my index finger, and said, *ein,* German for one. The baker gave me two. For the next choice, I spoke a bit louder. "*EIN.*" Again, she put two in the box.

The fourth time I received two instead of one, my children stifled their laughter and Matt explained. "Mom, Germans use their thumb for one and add the index finger for two, like this." Apparently, my gesture spoke louder to the baker than my pronunciation of *ein*. We spent a lot of money on pastries that day.

My best efforts at communication had failed.

Even when there's no language barrier, miscommunication can interfere with comprehension. Preconceived notions and unique speech patterns can skew a listener's understanding.

Speaking with God is different. He provides the gift of prayer as the means for two-way communication. No language barrier exists in conversations with our heavenly Father. He comprehends our thoughts, emotions, and utterances. He interprets voices raised in worship and hands lifted in praise. We can talk to Him with simple words or within our hearts when words won't come.

When we pray, we know God hears us and understands with perfection our imperfect prayers. We can pray with the psalmist, "I call upon you, for you will answer me, O God; incline your ear to me; hear my words" (Psalm 17:6).

Unlike some earthly parents who may remain distant or too busy to listen, God urges His children to come to Him. "Then you will call upon me and come and pray to me, and I will hear you. You will seek me and find me, when you seek me with all your heart" (Jeremiah 29:12-13). He expects us to come. He actually waits for us to come.

When I was a new believer, a friend suggested I ask God to teach me as I studied the Bible and talked with Him in prayer. She also advised I allow time to listen for His answers. In the Father's presence, I found comfort, wisdom, and help. The more I read and prayed, the more of His strength I had to combat doubt, fear, insecurity, and other spiritual enemies.

We can praise God for His mercy and faithfulness. Proclamations of thankfulness for His blessings fill our hearts and tumble out in words. In the privacy of a conversation with the Father, we can confess our sins and know He forgives us.

I'm thankful for Philippians 4:6 that teaches instead of allowing anxiety to rule my thoughts, I can share my burdens and requests

BEFORE, DURING, AND AFTER MEALTIME PRAYERS

During meal prep time, pray for your family, friends, and yourself.

When you pull up your chair to the table, thank God for His blessings.

While you clean the kitchen, pray for your church, neighbors, coworkers, and acquaintances.

with the Lord. "Do not be anxious about anything, but in everything by prayer and supplication with thanksgiving let your requests be made known to God."

We don't have to worry about where or when to pray. Jesus prayed at sunrise on mountainsides and late in a garden. David prayed in the pasture as a shepherd and in the palace as a king. We can approach God with confidence. He will always hear us.

We don't need a practiced verbal pattern or a menu of flowery words. No matter what language we speak, God understands us—the language of our heart, the words of a child speaking to our loving Father. What will you share with Him in prayer today?

*Then you will call upon me and come and pray to me, and I
will hear you. You will seek me and find me, when you seek
me with all your heart.*

Jeremiah 29:12-13

LET'S PRAY

*Most gracious Father, thank You for the gift of prayer. When I
hurry through my day and neglect our conversations, remind
me You are listening and long to teach me. I pray in the name
of Jesus. Amen.*

EMBRACING THE GIFT

You may want to organize a prayer binder with dividers for specific
people and needs. Date your requests and record God's answers.
Watch your faith and prayer life grow stronger as you read His responses later. When you study the Bible, write verses in your binder
you want to pray and weave them into your conversations with God.

SHARING THE GIFT

Pray Scripture this week for others' specific needs. Send texts, emails,
or handwritten notes to someone listed in your binder, and share the
verses you are praying for them.

the gift
of
TRANSFORMATION

Despite the steam-rising-from-the-asphalt heat of a July day, Tyler Marie and I stopped at Sweet Sue's Tearoom for lunch and a cup of hot tea.

I struggled to select a flavor. I love the heavenly aroma of cinnamon apple, but the tartness of black cherry is also appealing.

When the server came to our table, I ordered a new variety. "Cranberry-orange, please, and the Sue's Delight salad plate."

Sweet Sue's was one of those feel-good places that takes you back to simpler days with its eclectic furnishings and retro-café décor. "Mom, were the café signs like these when you were a little girl?"

I chuckled. "Yes, they were. Notice the prices. Twenty-five cents for a ham sandwich."

We paused our conversation when the server delivered our lunch, tea bags, pots of hot water, and delicate china teacups.

As I poured the steaming water over my teabag, a glorious red-orange hue began to seep from the teabag and diffuse the cranberry-orange flavor throughout the plain water. Its fruity aroma wafted across the table as I waited in anticipation for the steeping to be complete. The longer I waited, the richer the taste. The process reminded me of how Christ transforms our hearts.

Like steeping tea transforms hot water into an aromatic and delightful beverage, Christ transforms us from enemies of God, those who reject Him, into children of God and the aroma of Christ (Romans 5:10, 2 Corinthians 2:15).

I'm thankful our heavenly Father promises to continue His powerful work even after we become His children. What a comfort it is "that he who began a good work in you will bring it to completion at the day of Jesus Christ" (Philippians 1:6).

Each morning I look forward to steeping in God's Word and in prayer on my deck or nestled in my comfy bedroom chair. He speaks to my heart through the Bible, His Word, and changes me. I may not notice a definite message every day, but He teaches me more about His character and leads me to love and trust Him more. The more time I spend with Him in His Word, the more I notice our loving Father redirecting my thoughts and actions to align with His teaching.

Christ produces in us a deeper, more satisfying relationship with Him when we steep in His presence through time in the Bible and in prayer. The truths of Scripture swirl in our thinking and impart the goodness of God's Word.

Sometimes, I let myself steep in fear and worry rather than in the truth. What-if scenarios invade my thinking and magnify the uncertainty in my heart. But when I trust and obey God's Word, He fulfills His promise to guard my heart and mind. He proves Himself faithful—and He always will.

Recently, when several challenges led to anxiety and fear, the Holy Spirit reminded me of Philippians 4:6-7 where God teaches us not to fret but pray. "And the peace of God, which surpasses all understanding, will guard your hearts and your minds in Christ Jesus" (v. 7).

In the hot water of tough times, He's taught me the sweetness of trusting Him. I've learned when I come to Him for wisdom, He will remind me of biblical truth from a verse, a sermon, or a Bible study lesson that relieves my fears and helps me trust Him more—which pleases Him and brings me joy. Trials are still hard, and God doesn't

TABLE TIP

TRANSFORM LEFTOVERS INTO DELIGHTFUL DISHES

Melt shredded cheese over bits of chicken and combine with crisp veggies for a salad. Or use chunks of chicken to make a stir fry dinner. Preheat an electric skillet with olive oil. Add carrots and broccoli or frozen vegetables, peppers, onions, garlic, pepper, and a can of chicken and rice soup.

remove them all, but His Word will brew in us continually and develop a heart that turns to Him for help. A heart that chooses to walk through troublesome times with Him instead of choosing to fret or panic.

Remember, when we brew hot tea, the water doesn't enhance its own flavor. Instead, the tea infuses its richness throughout the water as the steeping process does its perfect work. God's gift of transformation is perfect work. Through it, He promises He will make us like Christ (Romans 8:29, Hebrews 13:21). He will make us a fragrant aroma—sweeter than the cranberry-orange tea at Sweet Sue's.

And I am sure of this, that he who began a good work in you
will bring it to completion
at the day of Jesus Christ.

Philippians 1:6

LET'S PRAY

Heavenly Father, thank You for the gift of transformation. I don't want to stay the same. I'm grateful for the work You began and faithfully continue to make me more like Jesus. Teach me through Your Word and renew my mind with Your Spirit's power. Rid my heart of any bitter taste of sin so that my words and actions testify of Your goodness. Transform me, I pray. Amen.

EMBRACING THE GIFT

Treat yourself to a cup of hot tea. Perhaps you want to try a new flavor. Consider it an example of the sweet truths God wants to give you in His Word. As you observe the way the tea transforms the water and imparts its flavor, ask God how He wants to change and teach you to make you more like Christ.

SHARING THE GIFT

Proverbs 27:17 reminds us "iron sharpens iron." Fellowship with other believers strengthens us and encourages us to open our hearts to the ways God wants to transform us. Set a time with a friend this week for a cup of tea and share what God has been teaching you as you've been steeping in His Word.

the gift
of GOD'S
JOY

Ray and I could see Mr. Horace standing at his open door as soon as we turned onto his dirt driveway. "Come on in," he said. "We've been waiting for y'all."

Aromas of country fried steak and creamed corn lured us into the kitchen where Mrs. Joann stood shaping biscuit dough. She wiped her hands and hugged us like long-lost relatives. Chuckling, she recalled the many biscuits she'd served my husband in his teen years. Mr. Horace and Mrs. Joann loved Ray like a son and had adopted me into their family soon after our engagement.

Despite health issues in their senior years, Mr. Horace repaired truck tires, and Mrs. Joann worked in a shirt factory. How could they be so joyful hosting us for dinner after working all day? I sometimes struggled to find joy during hard times.

During our previous visit, Mrs. Joann had served her county-famous chocolate pie with two-inch-high meringue. We'd laughed about the family stories Mr. Horace told while we savored every bite.

I'd never heard so much laughter from hard-working people with health concerns and meager means.

Joy seemed to percolate through their souls like the coffee I smelled brewing. An evening in a five-star restaurant with starched linens couldn't compete with the time we'd spent around this couple's oilcloth-covered table in their modest home. Joy shone from their faces like summer sunshine.

Today, the smell of food and the prospect of homemade dessert made me eager to pull up a chair to their table. Mrs. Joann called to her husband once the biscuits were done and the banana pudding meringue had browned. "Dinner's ready. Y'all come to the table while the biscuits are hot."

"Here we come," Mr. Horace said. "Time's a-wastin'."

Once we'd gathered around the table, he bowed his head. He spoke to God as if He were in the room with us. And He was. His prayer revealed their source of joy. Mr. Horace's words reflected a personal relationship with Christ as He thanked God for the food, the guests, their church—and the biscuits.

During dinner, the couple talked about what they'd learned in personal and church Bible study and how these truths influenced their lives. No wonder their hearts and home overflowed with joy—even in the face of challenging times. They chose the attitude of the prophet Habakkuk. "I will take joy in the God of my salvation" (Habakkuk 3:18).

From biscuits to banana pudding, we laughed and enjoyed sweet fellowship around Mr. Horace and Mrs. Joann's table. Their joy was contagious. After an evening in their home, I determined to spend more time in Bible study and to choose joy despite my circumstances. What beautiful examples of serving God with His gift of joy.

Centuries ago, a Philippian jailer exuded joy around his table after a startling event. While on guard duty, he woke up when an earthquake shook the prison's foundation. Cell doors swung open, and prisoners' chains broke. He grabbed his sword to commit suicide

TABLE TIP

THE-MORE-THE-MERRIER APPETIZER

Invite family and guests to share the joy of fellowship by creating an easy and attractive appetizer. Wash a large grapefruit, pat it dry, and place it on a plate. Cut a thin slice off the bottom to help it sit flat. Ask participants to spear the ingredients below onto toothpicks. Insert toothpicks all the way around the grapefruit.

· ½ inch cheese chunks

· tiny sweet gherkins or small kosher dill pickles

· olives with pimento

· maraschino cherries

Optional garnish: Arrange a thick ring of parsley around the base of the grapefruit. Picture perfect.

for fear of severe repercussions if the prisoners escaped. "Do not harm yourself, for we are all here," Paul cried out (Acts 16:25-28).

The stunned guard, who'd surely heard of Paul's testimony about Christ, asked, "Sirs, what must I do to be saved?" (vv. 29-30).

"Believe in the Lord Jesus, and you will be saved," Paul said, and the jailer did. Filled with the joy of Christ, he invited Paul and Silas to be his dinner guests, and "he rejoiced along with his entire household that he had believed in God" (vv. 31-34).

The joyous blessing of a relationship with Jesus permeated both our meal with our friends and Paul's meal with the Philippian jailer. Each gathering demonstrated that God's presence brings joy and protects us from discouragement when we face challenges and fearful moments.

Look around at the faces of people you encounter today and listen to their words. Perhaps they are waiting for a seat at your table where you can share the joy of Jesus—in good and difficult times.

And he rejoiced along with his entire household
that he had believed in God.

Acts 16:34

LET'S PRAY

Heavenly Father, thank You for the gift of joy we have in relationship with You. Help me fight the enemy of discouragement that threatens to overwhelm me in trying times. Guide me to share Your joy with those I meet. Amen.

EMBRACING THE GIFT

Write part of Nehemiah 8:10 on a card and post it in a conspicuous place. "The joy of the LORD is your strength." Each time you face potential joy-robbing situations, ask God to help you make the choice Habakkuk made. "I will take joy in the God of my salvation."

SHARING THE GIFT

We have opportunities to sow seeds of joy into the lives of others. Perhaps if we speak more of the blessings we experience and less of our problems, the joy of Christ will overflow our hearts and splash onto those around us. When we're tempted to complain, we can share pleasant news or tell how a Bible verse assures us of God's love and faithfulness instead. Then those around us will see the joy of the Lord in us.

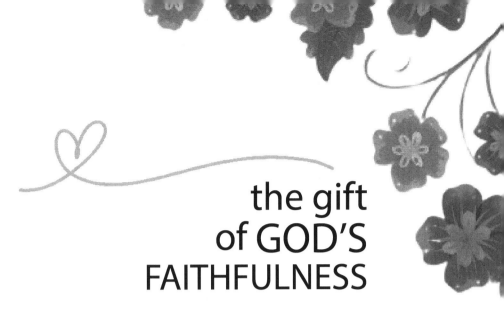

the gift of GOD'S FAITHFULNESS

My groom took my breath away. As I stood with him at the altar and the pastor asked the all-important questions, Ray's gaze met mine. "I do," we promised, "'til death do we part." Fifty years later, we're still smiling.

At our fiftieth anniversary celebration, Ray and I held hands at the table and reflected on decades of memories. We never could have dreamed of the joys—or challenges—we'd face.

We promised to love, honor, and cherish each other. "In sickness and in health, in poverty and in wealth." Our bank account reflected more poverty than wealth in our newlywed years.

Ray found a job near the college I attended, but Christmas tree prices sent us home empty-handed. Knowing my love of celebrations, my knight in shining armor climbed an ancient but unhealthy cedar tree on his family's land and cut off the top. Our little tree, wearing two strands of lights and a set of wooden ornaments I'd painted, made us rich—with joy.

With Ray's support, our marriage weathered my pursuit of three college degrees and both his challenging jobs and mine. He picked up take-out food, washed dishes and laundry, and returned countless library books while I studied and wrote papers. Each time the dean granted me a diploma, I felt like it should've read "Mr. and Mrs."

Ray and I navigated the happy—and choppy—waters of raising two children and shared parenting responsibilities. When I rocked sick babies at night, Ray cooked breakfast the next morning. His patience and gentle spirit calmed my mama's heart when I worried about the teenage years.

As he'd pledged, when I overcommitted to church and school activities, Ray stood by me, the queen of I-can-do-this-too. He *did* reel in my overzealous plans when he suspected they might overtax us. He guided by example and biblical truth. Ray's faithfulness reminds me of kept promises in another love story. A different kind of love story.

The widow Ruth pledged her loyalty to her mother-in-law Naomi. "For where you go I will go, and where you lodge I will lodge. Your people shall be my people, and your God my God" (Ruth 1:16). Ruth left her homeland and dedicated herself to her mother-in-law in Judah where the people worshiped the one true God.

The widows arrived in Bethlehem during the barley harvest (1:22). Ruth, according to custom, gleaned bits of grain the reapers left behind in the fields and brought them home to Naomi.

Boaz, the owner of one property, noticed Ruth and asked the manager of his workers about her. When he invited Ruth to continue working in his field and drink water from his well, she asked why.

"All that you have done for your mother-in-law since the death of your husband has been fully told to me, and how you left your father and mother and your native land and came to a people that you did not know before. The LORD repay you for what you have done, and a full reward be given you by the LORD, the God of Israel, under whose wings you have come to take refuge!" (2:11-12).

Boaz instructed his workers to sprinkle extra grain on the ground for Ruth. Her love and faithfulness to Naomi took his breath away. And he married her.

TABLE TIP

CELEBRATE FAITHFUL FRIENDSHIP

Find a recipe for Amish Friendship Bread. Most recipes require a starter, a mixture of yeast and baking ingredients which ferments. Preparation of a starter takes several days before it can be used or shared with others to start their batch of dough. If time is short, search for a recipe that doesn't require a starter. Invite friends for coffee and slices of your friendship bread. Share stories of friends who have remained faithful over the years or in hard times. Give each guest a copy of the recipe as a parting gift.

Greater than Ruth's or our faithfulness is the Lord's. "The steadfast love of the LORD never ceases; his mercies never come to an end; they are new every morning; great is your faithfulness" (Lamentations 3:22-23).

If we could interview heroes in the Bible, they would testify of God's steadfast love and faithfulness. Noah would advise dependency on God's promises, even in the face of monumental tasks. Daniel would praise God's protection in dangerous situations. Moses and Joseph would talk about God's constant presence, even in the desert seasons, from the pit to the palace. Peter would verify God's kept promise to forgive repentant hearts and honor flawed believers with kingdom work.

The better we know God's character through His Word, the more we embrace His gift of faithfulness and fend off the voices of fear, doubt, and worry. We can depend on His promises to guide, teach, and love us, to protect and forgive us. He is the God of kept promises.

The steadfast love of the LORD never ceases;
his mercies never come to an end;
they are new every morning; great is your faithfulness.
Lamentations 3:22-23

LET'S PRAY

Heavenly Father, great is Your faithfulness. When doubt and fear hound me, remind me to rest in Your love and trust the promises in Your Word. In the name of the One who is Faithful and True, I pray. Amen.

EMBRACING THE GIFT

Psalm 36:5 says of God, "Your steadfast love, O LORD, extends to the heavens, your faithfulness to the clouds." Take a picture of a cloud-filled sky and ponder the extent of God's faithfulness. Write the verse above in a journal or on a card and illustrate it with clouds to help you remember to thank God for His faithfulness.

SHARING THE GIFT

Faithfulness is one of the fruits the Holy Spirit produces in our lives (Galatians 5:22-23). With this Christlike trait, who can you serve this week to share and demonstrate His faithfulness?

the gift of GOD'S ACCEPTANCE

I dashed into the refuge of a restroom eight minutes before my appointment. Moisture dampened my palms, and I could barely swallow.

How could I face those PhDs? They only admit a handful into the doctoral program each year. I'm sure other applicants are more qualified. What will my colleagues at the college think if I'm rejected?

I could sneak past the door of the interview room, ride the elevator to the parking deck, and slip into my car. Surely, they'd had no-shows before.

Instead of bolting from the required interview for doctoral studies, I prayed.

"Father, I'm too nervous to go in there. Besides, they're not going to accept me anyway. But I *need* for them to accept me. Please help me."

The Holy Spirit brought Ephesians 1:6 to mind. "He made us accepted in the Beloved" (NKJV). Based on our response of faith in Jesus by God's grace, He accepts us in Christ, the Beloved of God, for His glory.

While I considered this powerful truth that God loves me and has already fully accepted me as His dear child, comfort and conviction permeated my heart.

I'd yearned for the approval of others. The words of Scripture pivoted my focus from people to God. He called me "accepted in the Beloved." I don't need the affirmation of others. I have Him, the God of the universe, as my Father.

I prayed some more.

"Father, I'll stay for the interview. If they reject me, I'll accept their decision as part of Your plan. Forgive me for allowing my desire for the approval of others to consume me. Thank You for reminding me I'm already accepted—by You. Thank You for the peace and joy You give me."

I tucked my arms to my sides to hide the perspiration rings from the morning, smiled, and entered the interview room. Confidence from a heavenly source welled up inside me.

Six professors who looked like they hadn't smiled since kindergarten sat at the long conference table like frozen statues, three on each side. The department chair pointed to my seat at the opposite end of the table.

They fired questions at me, and I answered. My voice didn't tremble, and my heart didn't race. One of my responses made their eyebrows arch, but God's comforting truth reverberated in my heart. *I am in Christ. I'm accepted by my heavenly Father.*

When the department chair dismissed me with, "Thank you, Mrs. Waters. You may leave," I felt like skipping down the gray-tiled hall. The cold demeanor of the committee members hadn't frozen my confidence. Their rapid-fire questions failed to generate panic. The likelihood of rejection hadn't flustered me. God's approval had defeated my fear of rejection.

A lady in the hall spoke to me as I pushed the elevator button. "You look happy today. You must have heard good news."

"Oh, I did," I said.

TABLE TIP

ACCEPTING AND WELCOMING OTHERS

Take time to welcome new neighbors, church visitors, new in-laws, or work colleagues. For snacks or meals, choose seats near the people who remain on the periphery of group conversations. Try the WELCOME acrostic below to offer acceptance.

Watch for opportunities to include everyone.

Establish eye contact to convey interest.

Look for ways to meet needs, such as sharing a meal.

Commit their names to memory.

Open your heart and pray for newcomers.

Meet them with a smile.

Express interest in their lives.

God's Word had filled me with comfort and the reminder of a precious gift—His acceptance.

Two weeks after I'd faced potential rejection at the conference table, I opened my acceptance letter from the university. I shared my decision with Ray. "The committee accepted me, but I'm refusing the offer. I've thought a lot about this doctoral program and realized it would demand too much time away from our family. I don't need the affirmation of others. I know now I only need the approval of One—our Father who's accepted me already."

After Ray's hug, I went into the bedroom. On my knees, I confessed to God my pride and misplaced dependence on the approval of people. I knew if I earned a doctoral degree, I'd gain prestige among my college colleagues. I'd seen it happen for others, and I'd imagined my new status as the solution for my insecurities. Filled with God's love, forgiveness, and acceptance, I praised Him.

Have you ever felt you needed—and depended on—the acceptance of others?

In Christ, His acceptance strengthens us to fight negative thoughts and feelings and stand against the desire to please others. We can enjoy our place at God's table—regardless of what happens around the conference tables of our lives. Reject the fear of rejection and embrace the acceptance of God. Then extend His grace to others.

He made us accepted in the Beloved.

Ephesians 1:6 NKJV

LET'S PRAY

Heavenly Father, thank You for accepting me as Your child. Forgive me for needing the approval of people. With Your love in me, I want to love and tell others about the acceptance they can receive in You. In the name of Jesus who loves us. Amen.

EMBRACING THE GIFT

When believers understand we're already accepted by God in Christ, the truth promotes confidence and makes a difference in our lives. Commit to trust Him and walk in confidence this week.

SHARING THE GIFT

God is honored when we accept others the way He accepts us. Romans 15:7 says, "Therefore receive one another, just as Christ also received us, to the glory of God." Look for opportunities to share the love of Jesus with someone. Greet newcomers to your church, workplace, or neighborhood with a smile and include them in conversation. A sincere welcome embraces others like a warm hug and builds bridges to the joy of acceptance.

the gift
of GOD'S
REST

Exhausted from work and travel, Ray and I climbed the steps of Dogwood Manor. The bed-and-breakfast served as our home away from home during our niece's wedding festivities.

The host greeted us with hot tea and crispy-thin lemon wafers. Then she escorted us to our suite filled with overstuffed chairs and lamplight. From the grandfather clock in the foyer to the four-poster bed, the furnishings welcomed us with warmth and comfort. Sleep came quickly.

The next morning at the dining table, we feasted on fruit, sausage, egg casserole, and fairy-sized biscuits with orange marmalade. Rest and the hearty meal fueled us to help with wedding preparations.

Elijah, the discouraged and terrified prophet of 1 Kings 19, didn't travel to a celebration like we did. He ran for his life. Queen Jezebel vowed to murder Elijah within twenty-four hours because he'd killed the evil prophets of Baal, a false god she worshipped (vv. 1-3).

When he'd escaped imminent danger, he accepted the meager amenities of a home away from home in the wilderness under a juniper tree. In despair, Elijah asked God to end his life and then slept, not in a four-poster bed, but on the ground (vv. 4-5).

His bed-and-breakfast host, an angel, told him, "Arise and eat." After he consumed hot bread and cool water, the tired prophet reclined again until the angel urged him to eat more (vv. 5-7).

Elijah "went in the strength of that food forty days and forty nights to Horeb, the mount of God," where he slept in his second B&B, a cave. Later, he met with the Lord (vv. 8-10). Knowing the human need for respite, God had allowed Elijah to sleep under the tree and in the cave before He revealed the prophet's next assignment (v. 15-16).

Whether we sleep in a magnificent inn or under the stars, we need pauses from our work. God's gift of rest strengthens us to fulfill the work He assigns. The psalmist understood the benefits. After he listed "green pastures" and "beside the still waters," he wrote of God, "He restores my soul" (Psalm 23:2-3).

Rest may be the most underused blessing God provides, yet Genesis 2:3 tells us He rested after six days of creation work. He instituted a day of Sabbath worship and relaxation for His people (Exodus 20:8). Although God denounces laziness in Proverbs 6:6, He commends rest.

Our hurry-scurry world drives us to work faster and longer. Instead of embracing God's Sabbath rest and taking a break on other days when we're tired, we sometimes continue the frantic pace or rob ourselves of sleep to get more done.

Our bodies, minds, and families suffer when we overtax ourselves. The National Center for Chronic Disease Prevention and Health Promotion connects the lack of sleep to heighted risk of some chronic diseases and includes the following warnings: "Not only are you more likely to feel sleepy, you're more likely to be in a bad mood, be less productive at work, and be involved in a motor vehicle crash." [1]

A QUICK AND TASTY
REST DAY LUNCH

Place ingredients in a crockpot and stir together.

½ package of frozen whole kernel corn (or 1 can)

1 can of black beans (drain or leave the liquid for a soupier dish)

½ package of taco seasoning or your own combination of spices

a medium or large jar of salsa, depending on preference

1-2 boneless chicken breasts or several tenders on top

Cook about 6 hours on low, depending on the size of the chicken.

Shred the chicken with a fork and stir.

Serve with your choice of cheese, lettuce, sour cream, guacamole, and tortilla chips.

Leftovers will freeze well for the next rest day.

—Recipe by Lori Hatcher

Adequate rest is a necessary protective gift from our heavenly Father. Without it, we can lose our ability to fight impatience, complacency, and irritability. Lack of rest may hinder effective service to Him. When we accept our need for respite, God blesses us with rest, both physical and spiritual. "It is in vain that you rise up early and go late to rest, eating the bread of anxious toil; for he gives to his beloved sleep" (Psalm 127:2).

Jesus's disciples worked in pairs to preach repentance, heal the sick, and cast out demons (Mark 6:7, 12-13). One day when they'd missed a meal, Jesus, recognizing the human need for rest, said to them and says to us, "Come away by yourselves to a desolate place and rest a while" (Mark 6:31).

Like the disciples and Elijah, we need times of renewal after ministry, demanding work, and the challenges of life. Jesus described the Sabbath as a gift from God. He said, "The Sabbath was made for man, not man for the Sabbath" (Mark 2:27).

God provides the gift of rest because He understands our need and wants us to worship Him. How are you resting?

Come away by yourselves to a desolate place and rest a while.

Mark 6:31

LET'S PRAY

Heavenly Father, thank You for the gift of rest. Help me balance work and rest as I serve You, my family, and others, and safeguard my health. Remind me to pause for times of prayer and refreshment with You, even when I'm busy. In Jesus's name I pray. Amen.

EMBRACING THE GIFT

Develop a habit of rest and prayer during the day. Stretch briefly and ask God to guide your work. Listen to a praise song when you take a break or walk outside to pray for refreshment and creativity.

SHARING THE GIFT

Encourage family members to turn off devices early, engage in a restful activity before bedtime, and go to bed without guilt over undone tasks.

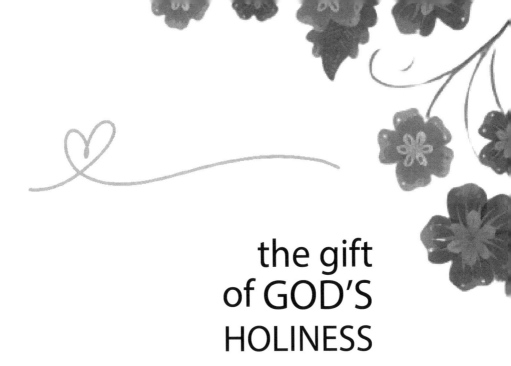

the gift
of GOD'S
HOLINESS

Before guest meals, Mama would say, "Let's get this silver cleaned ahead of time." Wearing rubber gloves, we'd scoop out a dollop of the gooey cleaner, smear it onto the silver, and polish with an old T-shirt.

Mama cleaned the large pieces, while I rubbed the sides of the sugar bowl and cream pitcher as if coaxing a genie from a lamp. We'd work until all the tarnish transferred to the cloth, and the silver sparkled under the hot water rinse. My favorite part of the job was smiling at my reflection in a shiny tray.

The sterling Rambler Rose flatware proved more challenging. Tarnish embedded itself in the embossed roses trailing down the handles. With elbows propped on the edge of the sink, I scrubbed, rinsed, and inspected each piece until the stubborn stain on the silver petals disappeared.

Silver polishing requires time and effort, but black-coated dishes and flatware look as disgusting as black-spotted lettuce in a salad or blue mold on dinner rolls. We want utensils and serving dishes—whether silver, china, or plastic—to be suitable for table service and as appealing to our dinner guests as the meal.

Just as Mama wanted spotless silverware on her table, God calls for spotlessness in his children. He calls it holiness. "You shall be holy, for I am holy" (1 Peter 1:15-16). God requires holiness, but it may seem impossible for sinners.

I'd have better success cleaning permanent marker stains out of a white wool sweater than I would removing the tarnish of sin from my life. As hard as I may try, I can't make myself holy. Only Christ can. "For our sake he [God] made him [Jesus] to be sin who knew no sin, so that in him we might become the righteousness of God" (2 Corinthians 5:21, brackets mine). On the cross, Jesus bore the guilt of our sin, and God applies the holiness of Christ to all who believe in Him.

What a marvelous gift.

It's as if God removes our ragged, stain-covered coat and replaces it with one so pure it shines like silver in the sunlight reflecting Christ's transforming work in our lives.

The Bible says believers become new creatures in Christ (2 Corinthians 5:17). We're changed. New. We have His characteristics. The holiness of Christ is one of the greatest gifts God gives those who believe in His Son.

Believers still fall to sin's temptations, but how thankful we are the polish of God's merciful forgiveness in response to our confession, cleanses sin's tarnish from our lives.

Jude said, "Now to him [Jesus] who is able to keep you from stumbling and to present you blameless before the presence of his glory with great joy to the only God, our Savior, through Jesus Christ our Lord, be glory, majesty, dominion, and authority, before all time and now and forever" (Jude 24-25).

Like Mama's clean silver tray gleamed on a table, polished hearts shine for Christ and please Him. Because God's standards are unattainable apart from belief in His Son, our generous Father has provided all we need through Him—even the holiness of Christ. His heart

TABLE TIP

A FRESH, WHITE TABLESCAPE

Perhaps change your table for dinner tonight by creating a fresh clean look. Consider a neutral-colored burlap table runner with a wide length of white lace down the center. You could add Mason jars to hold white flowers or greenery. Few people polish silver now, but if you have an old silver tray or bowl, you could polish it and place it or an old serving dish you rarely use on the table. Light some white pillar candles or add floating candles to a dish of water.

of love longs for us to enjoy His presence daily and seek His ways as He continues to make us more like Jesus.

After Mama and I polished silver to serve family and guests, we smiled at the results. Light sparkled off each piece and highlighted the metal's composition and reflective qualities. The gleam of clean silver dressed the table in finery and invited guests to pull up a chair.

When our lives honor Christ, the rays of His light dance from our lives and shine like silver. Most of all, we pray others will see the reflection of Him in us.

You shall be holy, for I am holy.

1 Peter 1:15-16

LET'S PRAY

Heavenly Father, I'm grateful for the gift of holiness. Purify my heart through Your Word and help me live in a way that honors You. Lead me to turn from sin that tarnishes my service to You. Shine the light of Jesus from my life as I seek to share Your love with others. In Jesus's name, I pray. Amen.

EMBRACING THE GIFT

The Bible says of believers, "Therefore, if anyone is in Christ, he is a new creation. The old has passed away; behold, the new has come" (2 Corinthians 5:17). With gratefulness in our hearts for this marvelous gift, we strive to walk in holiness as He continues His work in us.

When you're polishing silver, or more likely, treating stains on shirts or wiping counters clean, use these times to ask God to reveal any unconfessed sin or wrong motives in your heart. Agree with what He shows you and trust His forgiveness. Thank Him that He makes us fit for service in His kingdom.

SHARING THE GIFT

When you interact with others this week, pray for guidance and choose to shine with the holiness of Christ. What picture of Christ will those we meet notice in our actions, attitudes, and conversations?

the gift
of
GRATITUDE

While we sat around Aunt Tommie's pedestal oak table and sipped Coca-Colas, I grasped for every word of wisdom my eighty-five-year-old aunt shared.

"I don't understand why some old folks complain about people not coming to see them. They should find a hobby and be thankful for their blessings. Who wants to visit a whiny, old grouch? Why, I have plenty to keep myself busy. I call my friends, watch Atlanta Braves baseball, and paint a bit. And learning how to use my new laptop takes time. Not that I don't enjoy your visits, you understand. Come anytime you can."

My feisty aunt never whined. She made the best of each situation. When health issues reduced mobility, she watched more baseball on TV or invited her neighbor to visit. When cooking became difficult, she enrolled in a food delivery program and raved about the meals. The closest she came to a complaint was, "Some days lunch is tastier than others, but they bring a nice sandwich and a piece of fruit for supper."

Aunt Tommie expressed her opinions readily. "You choose to be thankful, or you choose to complain. We have too many blessings to complain about petty things."

That's how she saw it—as a simple choice.

Like my aunt's perspective, we have the same choice. When we read the Bible, we can choose to obey, or we can ignore what God teaches us. Two verses remind me to turn from complaining and thank Him. Philippians 2:14 says, "Do all things without grumbling or disputing." *All* things. Sounds like Aunt Tommie. Paul wrote in 1 Thessalonians 5:18, "Give thanks in all circumstances; for this is the will of God in Christ Jesus for you."

All circumstances.

When I visited Aunt Tommie, I patterned my speech after hers. I shared positive news or stayed quiet and listened because I wanted to get as much wisdom from this precious woman as I could in our time together.

The more time we spend with our heavenly Father and His Word, the more we learn from Him and want to please Him with our words. We want to imitate His character. Sometimes I find it hard to keep complaints to myself, like when other people's actions annoy me, or the weather is too hot or cold to suit me. Sometimes I'm tempted to talk more and listen less. I often pray, "Set a guard, O LORD, over my mouth; keep watch over the door of my lips!" (Psalm 141:3). Maybe Aunt Tommie prayed the same verse.

I'm thankful that when God tells us to do something, He enables us. By placing hearty portions of blessings on the table every day, paired with the wisdom and guidance of His Word, our loving Father equips us to honor Him with gratitude. He enables us to avoid the temptation to complain. Gratitude is an act of obedience and praise to the Giver of all good gifts (James 1:17). He gives believers the joy and privilege to express thanks to Him and influence others to be thankful too.

When God gives us a desire to break the complaint habit and develop a grateful heart, we can ask Him to forgive us and help us replace grumbling with thanksgiving. We can memorize Bible verses about praising God and avoiding complaints to help us remember. We can count our blessings like Aunt Tommie did and be grateful for what we have, not complain about what we think is missing.

The blessings on God's table lead us to honor Him with our thanks. We don't have to wait until November to start our gratitude list. We can begin today.

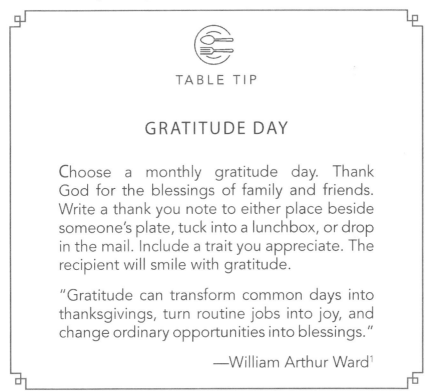

TABLE TIP

GRATITUDE DAY

Choose a monthly gratitude day. Thank God for the blessings of family and friends. Write a thank you note to either place beside someone's plate, tuck into a lunchbox, or drop in the mail. Include a trait you appreciate. The recipient will smile with gratitude.

"Gratitude can transform common days into thanksgivings, turn routine jobs into joy, and change ordinary opportunities into blessings."

—William Arthur Ward[1]

1. William Arthur Ward, Goodreads, Goodreads, Inc., 2023, https://www.goodreads.com/quotes/421800-gratitude-can-transform-common-days-into-thanksgivings-turn-routine-jobs, accessed February 12, 2023.

Give thanks in all circumstances; for this is the will of God in
Christ Jesus for you.

1 Thessalonians 5:18

LET'S PRAY

Heavenly Father, thank You for providing blessings that lead to praise and thanksgiving. Guard my lips against the temptation to complain and lead me to notice and appreciate Your blessings throughout each day. In the name of Jesus, I pray. Amen.

EMBRACING THE GIFT

When you're tempted to complain, stop and thank God for one of His many blessings. Ask a friend or family member to serve as an accountability partner for your speech and attitudes. Tell this person you want to thank God for His blessings and refrain from complaints. Choose Bible verses the two of you can read and memorize. The Holy Spirit will flash truth like caution lights to direct us away from ingratitude and toward thanksgiving.

SHARING THE GIFT

Write a list of people who have blessed you by their encouragement, faithful service, or their walk with Christ. Compose a note or an email to a few of them. Thank them for the difference they've made in your life and thank God for them. You may want to include someone who serves at your church or in a local business or medical office. When we express appreciation on a regular basis, we develop the habit of gratitude.

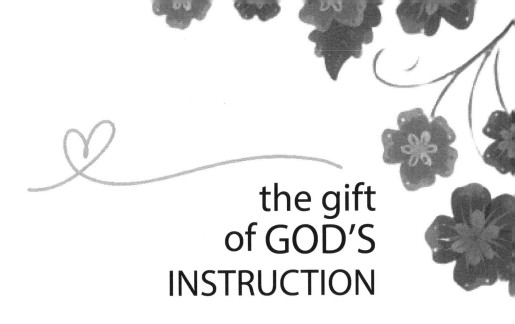

the gift
of GOD'S
INSTRUCTION

Pinch me, I must be dreaming.

Our family of four visited friends in Germany and accompanied them to the European Baptist Conference in Interlaken, Switzerland. Jungfrau, one of the highest peaks in the Swiss Alps, snow-capped in July, captured our attention while we unpacked our car at the conference site.

Swiss yodelers welcomed us as we gathered in the auditorium. We feasted on God's blessings through the music and stories of His miraculous work in the lives of people who trusted Him in difficult situations.

Dedicated missionaries and pastors led daily classes. They shared how God had changed their hearts, guided them, and met their needs. Love for Him and the people they served radiated from their faces and created in my heart a longing for a deeper walk with Jesus. I wanted to hear His correction and guidance more often. In prayer, I asked Him to teach me.

Messages during the general sessions that week fueled my faith. Classes about prayer and service equipped me. However, I learned the most valuable lessons in our chalet's charming dining room which doubled as my classroom. White lace curtains, fresh flowers on the tables, and the congeniality of fellow conferees brightened my mornings.

Some instruction came in the form of cards Frau Schoch, the chalet manager, had crafted. Each card contained a handwritten Bible verse and a picture she'd cut from a magazine. She placed one beside each plate every morning.

One verse on a colorful card comforted me about a personal concern and reminded me to trust God. On other days, I read verses about forgiveness, the need to encourage others, and how we must refrain from complaints—all lessons I needed. I tucked the cards into my Bible and thanked God for teaching me in creative and individual ways. His instruction corrects us, guides our steps, and protects us from false teaching and thinking our way is best.

One morning, I received a bonus lesson. Frau Schoch wiped her hands on her apron and prayed in English with a thick German accent. Then she invited us to help ourselves to as much food as we needed. The former missionary to impoverished people in Africa followed with a request. "Please do not waste the food God has given us."

I pondered her plea as I selected a boiled egg, fruit, a roll, and one link of sausage from the generous buffet. *She's right. Scripture teaches us to be good stewards of God's blessings. I try not to waste food, but how much do I throw away at home? Am I a good steward of God's blessings? Food, money, time, lessons from His Word?*

What valuable lessons I learned from the cards and words of Frau Schoch, a wise woman who'd studied the Bible and walked with God on two continents for decades. Our gracious Father continued to answer my prayer for correction and guidance all week.

The book of Proverbs highlights the importance of God's gift of instruction. "The fear of the LORD is the beginning of knowledge; fools despise wisdom and instruction" (1:7). "Listen to advice and accept instruction, that you may gain wisdom in the future" (19:20).

TABLE TIP

PASS A DISH OF INSTRUCTION

Invite a younger person to your house who's expressed interest in learning a skill you have, such as gardening, cooking, or creating a budget. Perhaps you know someone who wants to learn how to make a special dish or bake a dessert. Maybe they need help with marinade recipes and grilling techniques. You might copy several recipes or send them via email to a novice cook or newlywed.

I'd asked God to teach me at the conference. He did—through His Word and the examples of people who live according to the truths of Scripture. He used an unlikely trip and Bible verses on simple handmade cards to change my life.

The good news of Christ changed the lives of people Paul met on his missionary journeys. The early church in various locations learned biblical truth, as we do, through Paul's letters and preaching. We learn the identity of Jesus and how to honor Him with our lives.

Believers who met Paul, or read his letters, also learned by his example. In 1 Corinthians 11:1, he wrote, "Be imitators of me, as I am of Christ." Paul, a model of obedience, lived by God's Word even through danger and hardship. We learn God's instruction primarily through His Word.

I received more than breakfast at the chalet's dining table. God provided the spiritual nourishment I needed in the form of lessons from the Bible and godly examples. Frau Schoch's cards at my place setting on the table were a sweet example, but God places the gift of divine instruction on the table before us each day when we pray and read His Word.

Listen to advice and accept instruction, that you may gain wisdom in the future.

Proverbs 19:20

LET'S PRAY

Father God, open my eyes to everything You want to teach me today. You are my Teacher and the Giver of all good gifts, including Your instruction. In the name of Jesus, I pray. Amen.

EMBRACING THE GIFT

Read Psalm 32:8 about God's instruction. When you read the Bible, ask Him to correct and teach you. In a notebook or journal, date the page and write a few sentences about what you learn or copy a verse you want to remember. List your concerns and watch for His direction as you study and pray.

SHARING THE GIFT

Tell a friend about a lesson you learned from the Bible this week or share a verse you're studying. Pray for your friends to learn the lessons God uniquely designs for them.

the gift
of GOD'S
HOPE

My brothers and I ate every bite of the roast beef dinner my aunt prepared. We knew the prerequisite to gift opening was an almost clean plate.

While the adults lingered over coffee and fruitcake, we gobbled down star-shaped cookies and squirmed in the padded dining room chairs, necks craned toward the Christmas tree in the living room. I couldn't take my eyes off the sparkling packages. I hoped for a gift as special as last year's. Surely the grown-ups would finish soon.

After Aunt Eloise and Mama cleared the table, we gathered to open the presents.

Over the years, my brothers had opened watches, games, and a wood burning kit. I'd delighted in dolls, pajamas, and jewelry. Sparkly jewelry. My aunt's presents never disappointed us.

One year, when I picked up my gift, I heard high-pitched metallic notes. I'm sure my eyes widened when I tore open the wrapping to reveal the black jewelry box with pink roses painted on top. I thanked my aunt before I opened my treasure. "Oh, Aunt Eloise, I love it."

"Wait 'til you see what's inside," she said. I turned the music key on the bottom, opened the lid, and watched a tiny ballerina twirl and bounce to the tune of "The Skaters' Waltz." It was the best Christmas gift of all.

In ancient days, two of God's faithful servants waited with anticipation for the best gift of all time—the promised Messiah. Devout Simeon and Anna, an elderly prophetess, worshiped daily in the temple. With her hope fixed on God, Anna prayed night and day (Luke 2:36-37). Simeon prayed with great hope as he looked forward to "the consolation of Israel," their Messiah (Luke 2:25). For the hope God had given him "that he would not see death before he had seen the Lord's Christ" (v. 26). The One who would be called "Wonderful Counselor, Mighty God, Everlasting Father, Prince of Peace" (Isaiah 9:6).

When Jesus was born in Bethlehem, His young mother wrapped Him—God's long-awaited gift—in swaddling clothes and placed Him in a manger. When He was eight days old, Mary and Joseph traveled to the temple in Jerusalem "to present Him to the Lord" (v. 23).

Picture the scene in Luke 2 as Anna and Simeon gazed on the fulfillment of their hope. When Simeon entered the temple court, he may have halted when he noticed a young couple with a poor man's sacrifice—a pair of birds—for their infant Son's dedication.

Maybe the old man's heart skipped a beat and his eyes smiled when he realized the Child was the One he'd waited for. Perhaps his hands reached out for the infant Son of God. Tears of joy likely streamed down his wrinkled face as he cradled the Messiah he'd waited to see for so long.

Simeon blessed them but also spoke to Mary of the pain that would pierce her soul because of her Son (vv. 34-35)—a foreshadowing of Jesus's death. Anna lifted prayers of thanks to God and spoke to all who were waiting for the Christ (v. 38). She likely smiled at Mary and Joseph and gazed on the long-awaited Messiah through watery eyes, her age-spot-speckled hands lifted in praise.

For years, these two aging faithful ones had longed to witness the arrival of Immanuel. They'd waited with prayer, anticipation, and unfaltering confidence in God's promise.

Today, as followers of Christ, we live with assurance as we embrace the gifts of God because we have His gift of hope. Like Simeon and Anna, the promises of His Word fill us with the faithful hope of Christ. Paul's words speak a blessing to us. "May the God of hope fill you with all joy and peace in believing, so that by the power of the Holy Spirit you may abound in hope" (Romans 15:13).

TABLE TIP

BUDS OF HOPE

As a symbol of hope, plant flower bulbs in ceramic or terra cotta pots to use as a table centerpiece. Print Bible verses about hope to read each day as you wait for the first green shoots to appear. When flower buds appear, give one pot to someone who needs a reminder of God's hope and transplant the others to a flower bed or outdoor container. Suggested bulbs include amaryllis, paperwhites (narcissus), hyacinth, and daffodils.

NOTE: Research the growing season in your area. Make sure you place a plant saucer under each pot to protect your table when watering.

My brothers and I held onto the hope that Aunt Eloise's sparkling gifts would not disappoint. And they never did. Believers can trust every promise in God's Word with a deeper hope that never disappoints. While we long for the return of Christ, we trust He will come again just as He promised. Until then, let us follow the example of Simeon and Anna. Let us pray and watch for "our blessed hope, the appearing of the glory of our great God and Savior Jesus Christ" (Titus 2:13).

May the God of hope fill you with all joy
and peace in believing,
so that by the power of the Holy Spirit
you may abound in hope.

Romans 15:13

LET'S PRAY

Heavenly Father, thank You for the hope I have in You—glorious hope for each day and the hope of Your coming. Help me trust You more until You bring me to my eternal home with You. In Jesus's name, I pray. Amen.

EMBRACING THE GIFT

The more we study the Bible, the more our hope grows and matures. We can proclaim with confidence, "Let us hold fast the confession of our hope without wavering, for he who promised is faithful" (Hebrews 10:23). Do you need hope for situations in your life? Write them down and pray for God to give you hope and wisdom. Add verses you read about God's faithfulness and hope.

SHARING THE GIFT

Copy Romans 15:13 and paste it into the Notes app on your phone or write it onto a notecard and tuck it in your purse. If a friend sounds hopeless or needs encouragement to trust God, you could send the verse to her in a text, email, or card, and include your promise to pray.

the gift
of
SERVICE

Butterflies danced in my stomach. I'd never taken a sewing class before, but I wanted to create beautiful accessories for my home, so I signed up. Now I was in trouble. Big trouble.

Everyone around the table knew more about sewing than me. My fabric projects included one pair of kitchen curtains and thirty bean-bags I'd made for my classroom decades ago.

When the instructor asked the class to prepare bobbins and thread their machines, my butterflies fluttered so much they could have churned butter. I only knew bobbins as little round gizmos hidden in a secret compartment of the machine.

"Raise your hand if you need help," the instructor said.

I raised my hand as fast as a kid when Mom asks, "Who wants dessert?"

"What's giving you trouble?"

I answered with a sheepish grin. "Um, I don't how to thread the sewing machine. And I can't find the feed dogs you mentioned."

Without speaking a word or making eye contact, she threaded my machine, inserted a bobbin with matching thread, and moved on to distribute instruction sheets to the class. These were equally confusing with terms like *cross grain* and *grade the seam.*

I turned toward a kind-looking woman. "Could you help me get started, please?"

"Sure. Let me take my bobbin out, and I'll move to the empty machine beside you." My hyperventilating butterflies breathed a sigh of relief.

Becky and I worked together, side-by-side, for the next two hours to make our table runners. Other women left with their finished products, but Becky continued to help me. Maybe she needed to run errands or cook dinner, but she'd tucked the gifts of service and patience into the seams of her assistance.

When we finished the final seams, we admired our handiwork, turned out the lights, and walked down the hall. "Thank you so much, Becky. Without you, I would have left at the beginning."

She smiled and hugged me when we reached the parking lot. "I was happy to help. I'll tell you a little secret. Last Sunday our pastor taught us about serving God by serving others. Sometimes I'm more focused on my needs than the needs of those around me. I asked God to give me an opportunity to serve someone this week, and He did. He gave me you, and I'm grateful."

My butterflies waltzed ahead of me and fluttered away. I climbed into my car and thanked God for Becky, a modern-day Dorcas.

Dorcas was a seamstress and much-loved follower of Christ who lived in Joppa. She excelled in doing good for others before she became ill and died. Overcome with grief, her friends sent for Peter. When he arrived, "the widows stood beside him weeping and showing tunics and other garments that Dorcas made while she was with them" (Acts 9:39). After Peter prayed, God restored her life, and she sat up. The joyous news "became known throughout all Joppa, and many believed in the Lord" (v. 42).

God's Spirit produces a desire to serve in the hearts of believers, and He leads us to reach out to others. Jesus reminded His squabbling,

TABLE TIP

BLESSING BAG LUNCHES TO GO

Prepare bag lunches (or trays of food) for workers on a mission project or at a service organization. Suggested items include sandwiches, chips, fruit, carrot sticks, and cookies. You could add a thank-you-for-your-service card with a Bible verse if you like.

self-serving disciples of this when He said, "If anyone would be first, he must be last of all and servant of all" (Mark 9:35).

Serving doesn't have to be complicated or elaborate. While God might call us to dedicate several hours of time as Becky did in the sewing class, oftentimes simple gestures mean the most. My friend Lori held an umbrella over a young couple waiting in a downpour after a car accident and offered to pray with them. Jean planned movie nights for a neighbor enduring cancer treatment. Ladies at our church fashioned sleep mats out of plastic bags for homeless people. Like Becky and Dorcas, these women served others out of the overflow of their love for God.

My new friend Becky's help reminded me to never underestimate the value of a simple act of service to calm another person's butterflies or meet a need—even when it involves mysterious bobbins and table runners.

If anyone would be first, he must
be last of all and servant of all.
Mark 9:35

LET'S PRAY

Thank You, Father, for the times you've allowed me to serve You by serving others. And thank You for the times you've moved others to serve me. Help me become more like Jesus so service will come naturally and joyfully—even when it's hard. In His name, I pray. Amen.

EMBRACING THE GIFT

Notice those who serve others at your church or in your community. Tell them you appreciate their work. Then thank God for the talents, skills, knowledge, or experience He's given you so you can serve Him by serving others.

SHARING THE GIFT

Pray for guidance and explore service opportunities in your community. You might serve meals at a local soup kitchen or volunteer at a ministry's thrift store or clothing bank. Does a military family in your church or neighborhood need help with home repairs or childcare? Maybe you could serve as a volunteer tutor or mentor at a local school. Ministries at your church may need additional workers.

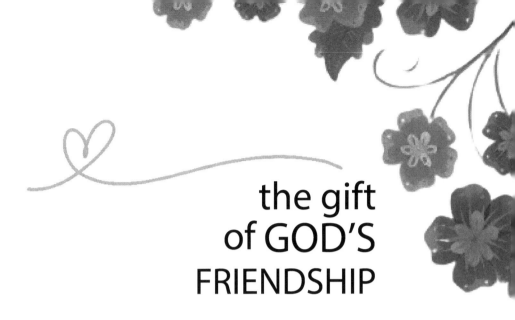

the gift of GOD'S FRIENDSHIP

Puzzled by his daughter Chelsea's request, my brother Carson asked, "You want us to deliver three tables and twelve dining room chairs to where? The beach?"

"Yes, Dad," she said, "and can you please hurry? Josh promised to help, but his boss called him to work. We need the tables and chairs on the beach by 8:30 so we'll have time to set up."

"May I ask why?"

"Laura and I are giving a bridesmaids' brunch on the beach for our friend Jacqueline. Can you get there by 8:30?"

"Sure, no problem," Carson said, shaking his head and smiling.

My servant-hearted brother called a friend with a truck, loaded the furniture, and drove to the beach.

Under a blue-sky canopy, Chelsea and Laura spread a tarp as a carpet over the sand and directed the furniture placement. Then they set to work.

They tied blue ribbons around Mason jars and filled them with sunflowers and delphinium. The girls set the tables with china plates, linen napkins, and silverware. After checking the ham biscuits and blueberry muffins in their thermal bag, they placed bowls of strawberries and trays of cantaloupe slices on the table. Then they poured orange juice and waited for the honoree.

Sunlight sparkled on the ocean like diamonds. The call of seagulls and the crash of waves morphed into background music as the chattering guests gathered in the elegant outdoor setting.

When the celebration ended, the bride thanked her hosts. "This was so much fun. After the busyness of planning, I loved relaxing at the beach and visiting with friends. You two mean the world to me. Your friendship is one of God's best blessings in my life."

After multiple hugs, Jacqueline left the beach to prepare for her wedding.

Chelsea and Laura high-fived each other. Mission accomplished.

In a demonstration of supreme love and obedience to the Father's plan, Jesus accomplished His mission on the cross. "Greater love has no one than this, that someone lay down his life for his friends" (John 15:13).

Jesus calls believers friends in John 15:14-15. "You are my friends if you do what I command you. No longer do I call you servants. . . . I have called you friends, for all that I have heard from my Father I have made known to you." By His crucifixion and constant presence with us, Jesus proves His sovereign power and His tender love. Our holy, almighty God is also our loving Friend.

The apostle Paul teaches us to imitate Christ in the way He shows love. "Therefore be imitators of God, as beloved children. And walk in love, as Christ loved us and gave himself up for us, a fragrant offering and sacrifice to God" (Ephesians 5:1-2). When we imitate Christ, we can be a friend who "loves at all times" (Proverbs 17:17).

With God's love in our hearts, we can share His love in the bonds of friendship with others like David and King Saul's son Jonathan did. David spoke with the king after he'd slain the giant Philistine. "As soon as he had finished speaking to Saul, the soul of Jonathan was knit to the soul of David, and Jonathan loved him as his own soul" (1 Samuel 18:1).

TABLE TIP

FORGET-ME-NOT FRIENDSHIPS

Plant forget-me-not flower seeds in a pretty flowerpot. When the seeds sprout and grow, use the plants as a centerpiece on your table and as a reminder of the gift of friendship with Christ and others. When the tiny plants break the surface, present them as a gift to a friend. Glue the seed package onto the front of a handmade card. Include a note like this one: "I'll never forget the blessing of your friendship. 'A friend loves at all times'" (Proverbs 17:17).

Scripture teaches us how to forge godly friendships like theirs. "Therefore encourage one another and build one another up, just as you are doing" (1 Thessalonians 5:11). "Love one another with brotherly affection. Outdo one another in showing honor" (Romans 12:10).

The gift of friendship draws us close to Christ and each other and gets us through tough and good times. You may not be at the beach with friends today but pull up a chair to your breakfast table. Picture Jesus sitting across from you, offering the blessings of His friendship along with daily provision. As you leave the table, what difference will His friendship make in your life and in the lives of those you meet?

No longer do I call you servants ... I have called you friends,
for all that I have heard from
my Father I have made known to you.

John 15:15

LET'S PRAY

Heavenly Father, thank You for Jesus's perfect example of friendship. Help me to obey You and reflect Your love to my friends and to those I don't know well. Make me a friend who loves at all times, one who speaks edifying words to others. Guide me to share Your love and the gift of friendship with someone today. Amen.

EMBRACING THE GIFT

If you know Jesus as your Savior, also think of Him as a friend this week. How do you think your prayer time will change? Ponder this question: How can Jesus's example make us a better friend to others?

Perhaps you've never accepted Jesus's invitation of salvation and eternal life. He's the Friend who promises to never leave you (Hebrews 13:5). Romans 10:9 says, "If you confess with your mouth that Jesus is Lord and believe in your heart that God raised him from the dead, you will be saved."

SHARING THE GIFT

Ask God to lead you to someone who needs your friendship this week. Perhaps you could invite that person to join you for a meal or cup of coffee for the purpose of extending love and companionship. Pray about sharing your relationship with Jesus.

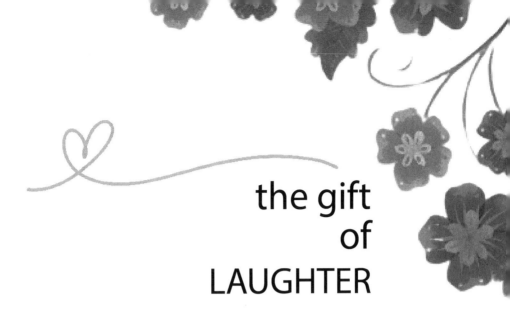

the gift
of
LAUGHTER

As a child, my like-a-sister friend Karen dreamed of being a mother. She rocked her baby dolls and pretended to feed them at her child-sized table. When asked, "What will you be when you grow up?" she'd answer, "A mommy."

For the first ten years of Karen and Gene's marriage, she longed for a baby but endured disappointment and heartache. She dreaded the Mother's Day celebrations at church when children presented long-stemmed carnations to their moms. Karen served dinner in front of the television to avoid envisioning children around their dining table. She smiled at baby showers but ached with longing.

Infertility crushed her dreams.

Even in her deep disappointment, though, Karen knew God's plans are best. Yet, she struggled to embrace them. She prayed she'd honor Him and determined to love everyone God placed in her life.

She sang in the church choir, directed the children's choir, and babysat for young families. At church, calls of "Hey, Mrs. Karen" echoed through the halls as children ran to hug her. But sometimes the longing felt crippling—until the day God worked through a five-year-old boy and a carnation.

At church one Mother's Day, our five-year-old son, Matt, chose two long-stemmed carnations—one for me and one for Karen. When he said, "For my second mom," tears rolled down her cheeks. He hugged her. "I thought you liked flowers." Laughter replaced her tears. Healing laughter.

Matt rode to lunch with Gene and Karen every Sunday after church. He'd noticed how they referred to each other as "Dear." One Sunday, he asked Gene, "Mr. Dear, could I ride with you and Mrs. Dear?" Karen and Gene laughed.

God used Matt's gift of a flower to break through Karen's sorrow and enable her again to embrace His gift of laughter. To trust God's faithfulness and discover that pain released to Jesus bears joyful fruit. In later years, she delighted in her niece and nephew. Today she laughs, rather than mourns, when visiting children, like Michael Robert, her precious grandnephew.

Thousands of years ago, another woman longed to be a mom. When she was sixty-five, God promised Abraham and his barren wife Sarah, He'd give them a son. Sarah's hope had soared, but twenty-five years later, that hope dwindled when she remained childless.

When she was ninety, God repeated His promise to Abraham. Sarah laughed, but not with faith-filled laughter from abiding trust. Mocking laughter of unbelief.

God said to Abraham, "Is anything too hard for the LORD? At the appointed time I will return to you, about this time next year, and Sarah shall have a son" (Genesis 18:14).

And she did.

As God had promised, Sarah gave birth to a son. Abraham named him Isaac, the Hebrew word for laughter.

Imagine the joy that bubbled into laughter from the depth of Sarah's soul. "God has made laughter for me; everyone who hears will laugh over me" (Genesis 21:6).

TABLE TIP

LAUGHTER IS GOOD MEDICINE

Laughter is good medicine, especially during or after challenging times. Place a funny card or comic strip beside someone's plate when they need a laugh. Start a 'Laughter Jar' and decorate it with smiles. Encourage family or guests to describe on a strip of paper a time they laughed at themselves. Put the strips in the jar. Once a year, open the jar during a meal. Let each person read their notes and laugh again.

Unlike Sarah, God never gave Karen a child of her own, but every day He fills her heart with peace and contentment in Him and opportunities to serve the children and adults He sends to her to love.

Karen learned God's gift of laughter isn't only for those who receive all their dreams. Like her, we can embrace laughter even in deep disappointment when we understand the joy we have in the Lord. When we trust God and serve—and laugh with—those He sends us to love.

If you asked Karen, "Is anything too hard for the LORD?" she would answer, "No! Nothing is too difficult for Him. He is enough."

God has made laughter for me; everyone
who hears will laugh over me.

Genesis 21:6

LET'S PRAY

Father, when I focus on what I lack, I allow pain and disappointment to paralyze me. Help me trust You enough to embrace Your gift of laughter, even in my pain. Help me use Your gifts to serve You and the people You send to me. Show me ways to share the joy of knowing You and Your gift of laughter with those around me. Amen.

EMBRACING THE GIFT

Are you facing heartache or disappointment? Has laughter left your heart or home? Read 1 Peter 1:3-9 and write a prayer of thanks for the "imperishable, undefiled, and unfading" promises God has preserved for all who trust in His Son—because He loves you (Isaiah 43:4). Look each day for evidence of God's faithful love for you and pass it on to the next person you meet.

SHARING THE GIFT

According to the Mayo Clinic, laughter can increase oxygen intake, decrease heart rate, and improve circulation. It can reduce pain and make challenging situations easier. [2] God knew this.

A joyful heart is good medicine,
but a crushed spirit dries up the bones.

Proverbs 17:22

A PLACE AT HIS TABLE

When appropriate, encourage laughter to brighten the day for someone who's lonely or in a difficult circumstance. Share a humorous story, comic strip, or funny card to bring a smile to someone's face.

the gift
of GOD'S
GENEROSITY

On University of Georgia game days, Ray and I enjoyed a tailgate feast of fried chicken, pimento cheese sandwiches, chips, and fruit. One year, after the first game of the season, Tyler Marie called. "Hey, Mom, mind if I bring some friends to tailgate for the next game?"

"That would be fine. We'd love having them. How many?"

"I'm not sure yet," she said, "but I'll let you know."

She called mid-week to tell us two of her friends planned to join us.

Avid Bulldog fans, we dressed our portable table with a black and white checked tablecloth, red pom poms, and a ceramic bulldog centerpiece. We listened to the pre-game show on the radio and the Georgia Redcoat Marching Band in the distance while we arranged the food.

When the three students arrived, Ray welcomed them and led them to the table. "Fill up your plates and come back for seconds. We have plenty."

After we ate, we walked to the game. "Madison and Lindsey want to tailgate with us next time too," Tyler Marie said. "Is that okay?"

"The more the merrier," Ray and I said almost in unison and laughed.

Two weeks later, at the next home game, six students joined us. While we visited, I asked about their favorite foods, and our future menu expanded. We added sweet tea, potato salad, and banana pudding.

After I calculated the food cost for our growing group, I brainstormed ways to be frugal. I suggested we make more sandwiches and buy less chicken. Instead, Ray encouraged me to increase the amount of chicken we normally bought. "Those college students don't eat breakfast before they come, and they'll be starving," he said. "Let's make baked beans and cookies too." His generosity made me smile.

Our picnic meal transitioned into an al fresco smorgasbord. We always had more than we needed, but Tyler Marie and her roommates loved the leftovers. The hugs and fun we shared around the table created memories more precious than the cost of the meals. The number of students varied with each remaining home game, but we enjoyed serving as many as twelve. Our love for our daughter and her friends motivated us to serve generous amounts of food and hospitality.

Jesus once served an al fresco meal to 5,000 men and their families who'd listened to His teaching all day (Luke 9:10-17). Finding only meager amounts of food in the crowd, His disciples urged Him to send the people into nearby villages to eat. Instead, Jesus demonstrated His power and His generous heart. "And taking the five loaves and the two fish, he looked up to heaven and said a blessing over them. Then he broke the loaves and gave them to the disciples to set before the crowd. And they all ate and were satisfied" (vv. 16-17).

The generous amount Jesus provided fed thousands of people, and like our tailgate meal, there were leftovers—twelve baskets of them (v. 17).

Ray and I enjoyed sharing generous amounts of food with our daughter and her friends. Imagine God's joy in providing for His children with much greater love and generosity than human parents. He doesn't fill our plates from a bread-and-water-only pantry, but from His unlimited stores of heavenly wealth. He meets our physical and spiritual needs with His gift of generosity.

When I read the account of Jesus feeding the multitude, I wonder why He created extra fish and bread instead of the exact amount. He's omniscient and would have known exactly, to the ounce, how much each person would eat. I don't know the size of the baskets the disciples used, but they filled twelve with leftovers.

God's blessing provided what the crowd needed and more. Could the account of this miracle include a lesson about His generosity? He always meets our need and often gives us extra—enough to share with others—not leftovers to waste, but treasures overflowing from His generous heart to bless others. Jesus said, "It is more blessed to give than to receive" (Acts 20:35). We follow His example when we give, whether from a large or small supply.

Tyler Marie and her friends learned to trust us for pre-game food. In a much deeper way, and with more certainty, we learn to trust

TABLE TIP

DOUBLE THE BLESSING

Place a **G** beside some of the non-perishable items on your grocery list. Buy two of each item with a **G** and place them in a 'Generosity' box or bag when you get home. Look for advertised non-perishable BOGO items. Donate the contents to a local food bank or ministry. You may choose to volunteer your time to help when you drop off the food.

God's generosity. He provides for our physical needs and lavishes us with His love, grace, forgiveness, and other blessings—enough to share. As surely as Jesus multiplied the loaves and fish, He can grow our generosity and the desire to bless others.

It is more blessed to give than to receive.

Acts 20:35

LET'S PRAY

Gracious Father, thank You for meeting my needs and pouring extra blessings into my life. Fill my heart with Your generosity and show me how to share with others. Amen.

EMBRACING THE GIFT

Try the "Three P's of Generosity."

Prepare. Prepare your heart by reading about God's generosity (Romans 8:32, John 10:10, Ephesians 1:3).

Praise. Praise God for His blessings and opportunities to give.

Pray. Thank God for His generous heart and ask Him to make you a cheerful giver.

SHARING THE GIFT

Ask God for opportunities to share His generosity with others, then watch for needs around you. Could you share a meal with an elderly person or take donations to a food bank? You may give from your financial blessings or spend your time with someone who needs companionship. Could you sing, take flowers, or share a devotion with patients at a nursing facility? Generosity of all kinds models the heart of Christ to those around us.

the gift
of GOD'S
COMFORT

When my mom, Tyler Marie, and I reached our vacation destination in Edinburgh, the cab driver's words alarmed us. "Aye, what you heard is true. A troublesome group plans to protest the inter-governmental meeting scheduled near the city later this week. I'd stay close to the hotel if I were you."

Threats of political unrest and violence unsettled our party of three. The desk clerk confirmed the news.

Anxious and hesitant to venture too far from the hotel before getting more information, we wandered into a quaint tearoom tucked into an adjacent alley or *close,* as the Scots say. White lace curtains covered the windows, and handmade items adorned the cornflower blue walls. Small round tables with chairs filled the cozy room.

Christine, the charming white-haired owner, greeted us with a smile and twinkling blue eyes. She listened to our concerns and assured us the Edinburgh police could manage any disturbance that might erupt. Then, Christine shifted the conversation to the parts of her beautiful country we should visit. We listened while she sketched a map and gave directions.

Comfort seemed to waft through the room like the aroma of the hot tea we sipped while nibbling on freshly baked blueberry scones. With calmer hearts, we walked back to our hotel room and prayed for safety before climbing into bed.

The next morning, we followed Christine's advice to skirt the downtown protests. We toured a castle and joined a bus tour to the scenic highlands. Back in Edinburgh and exhausted from our sightseeing ventures, we returned to the cozy tearoom, our home away from home at an anxious time.

When anxiety threatens to unravel our peace, we find our hearts' home away from home when we talk with God in prayer. We can tell Him what unsettles us and depend on His help through the comforting words of the Bible and wise counsel from other people.

In challenging times, we often long for a reprieve, a peaceful shelter free of nagging worries and fears. Supportive friends and loved ones reassure us, but sometimes our need burrows deeper than human beings can reach or solve. These long-lasting concerns entrenched deep in our hearts seem inescapable, almost taking up permanent residence. Strategies and self-help efforts fail or provide only short-term relief, but Psalm 94:19 reassures us. "When the cares of my heart are many, your consolations cheer my soul."

In the Scottish tearoom we found temporary consolation, but our gracious Lord places generous portions of comfort on His table every day. He is the only One who can alleviate our deep fears, doubts, and worries, even if troubling circumstances persist. The apostle Paul called Him "the Father of mercies and God of all comfort" (2 Corinthians 1:3). Then, in verse four, Paul gives us one of the reasons God calms our hearts: "so that we may be able to comfort those who are in any affliction, with the comfort with which we ourselves are comforted by God." What a privilege to share this precious gift with others.

Sometimes when I need comfort, I steep tea in the porcelain cup I purchased in the Scottish tearoom. Then I curl up in a chair with my Bible and talk with my Father. I often read the soothing words of

EASY AND COMFORTING
VEGETABLE SOUP

Cut pre-cooked beef tips into bite-sized pieces.

Chop and add onions, carrots, and celery.

Add two cans of diced tomatoes and a can of corn, all undrained.

You may add butterbeans, cut green beans, or peas.

Add water to create desired thickness, and season as desired.

Simmer on low. During the last few minutes, add diced potatoes and barley.

Double the recipe and store half of it in the freezer for a delightful dinner on a busy night or share with a family who would appreciate a meal.

Philippians 4:6-7. "Do not be anxious about anything, but in everything by prayer and supplication with thanksgiving let your requests be made known to God. And the peace of God, which surpasses all understanding, will guard your hearts and your minds in Christ Jesus."

He is the God of all comfort.

*Blessed be the God and Father of our Lord Jesus Christ,
the Father of mercies and God of all comfort.*

2 Corinthians 1:3

LET'S PRAY

*Heavenly Father, thank You for being my Comforter. When
I try various means to soothe hurts and fears, please whisper
Your love to me and remind me that only You provide deep,
welcomed relief. Show me, Father, how to share Your consolation with others this week. In Jesus's name, I pray. Amen.*

EMBRACING THE GIFT

Write a list of your fears and worries and brew a cup of tea or coffee. As you wrap your hands around the warm cup, read 2 Corinthians 1:3-4. Ask God to calm your anxious heart and fill you with the
warmth of His comfort. When I read in the Psalms and talk with our
heavenly Father, my anxious heart settles. I'm praying you'll find His
comfort, dear reader.

SHARING THE GIFT

Maybe you'll have an opportunity to share God's comfort this week.
A friend may be anxious about a medical diagnosis or an upcoming
test. A loved one may struggle to balance work and homelife. Grief
may be overwhelming a neighbor or coworker. You could share encouragement in a conversation or with a handwritten note in a card.
Include verses you've come to treasure about the Lord's comfort.

the gift
of GOD'S
GRACE

My body jolted from the head-on collision. Distracted by thoughts of my mom's recent diagnosis, I'd exited the interstate and turned the wrong way onto a one-way street.

"God, please help me," I prayed as steam erupted from my crumpled car. "Look what I did. Please let the other driver be okay. Oh, Father, please help us."

I released the breath I'd been holding when I saw the other driver exit his car and walk toward me. "Are you okay?" I sputtered through my car window while I fumbled for my cell phone to call my husband. "I drove the wrong way. I'm so sorry. Please forgive me."

The kind man smiled. "I'm fine. I'm glad *you* weren't hurt."

We had escaped unscathed, and the man I hit responded with grace instead of a barrage of angry accusations.

"Thank You, Father," I whispered under my breath. Moments after I climbed from the car on wobbly legs, Ray arrived.

He hugged me, and a geyser of tears erupted from my pool of relief and regret. As we drove to the hospital in a second attempt to visit my mother, he patted my shoulder and listened to my play-by-play account of the accident.

"We all make mistakes, Jeannie," he said.

It wasn't until we joined my brother Ed and his wife, Suzanne, at a hospital cafeteria table that I inhaled my first deep, post-accident breath. "It was my fault," I said. "I can't believe I did that. That man could have been seriously injured, but he was so kind."

Ed spoke words that soothed my soul. "You were wrong. You caused the accident, but it wasn't intentional. You can buy a new car, but I can't get another sister. I'm thankful you're okay." My brother's words assured me that although I'd broken a traffic law, no one condemned me. Instead, everyone involved had extended grace.

Suzanne echoed his affirmation. "Jeannie, we're just thankful no one was hurt. You're much more important to us than a car." More grace.

I'm grateful God provides grace as a gift to His children. Sometimes it comes straight from His heart to ours. Other times He uses kind people like Ray, the other driver, or my brother and sister-in-law to deliver it.

In the book of Joshua, as the Israelites stood poised to conquer the city of Jericho, God extended grace to one faith-filled woman and her family.

Rahab, like the other residents of Jericho, deserved God's judgment. She had worshiped the false gods of her countrymen and lived as a prostitute. Yet her heart quickened when she heard of the miracles the God of the Israelites had done. When three Israelite spies appeared at her doorstep, she pled her case.

"Please swear to me by the LORD that, as I have dealt kindly with you, you also will deal kindly with my father's house, and give me a sure sign that you will save alive my father and mother, my brothers and sisters, and all who belong to them, and deliver our lives from death" (Joshua 2:12-13).

In an outpouring of grace that came straight from God, the spies assured her they would spare hers and her family's lives. "Our life for yours even to death! If you do not tell this business of ours, then

A GRACE MEAL

Thank God for grace and His blessings we can't secure for ourselves. Extend a dinner invitation to someone who may be unable to reciprocate. Consider a single mom, widow or widower, a person who is physically unable to cook or a family who would enjoy a meal around your table.

when the LORD gives us the land we will deal kindly and faithfully with you" (v. 14).

Rahab didn't deserve such grace. Neither did I when I crashed my car into that poor unsuspecting man's vehicle. Which is the whole point of grace. If we could earn it or deserve it, it wouldn't be grace.

The psalmist's description of God's character tells us this gift originates in the heart of our heavenly Father. "The LORD is merciful and gracious, slow to anger and abounding in steadfast love" (Psalm 103:8). Amazed by God's grace and the countless times other people have extended it to us, we long to share this blessing.

When I remember those awful moments after my accident, and, on a much more serious scale, think about Rahab the prostitute, I marvel anew at the grace God freely gives His children. This knowledge makes me want to be a grace bearer too.

The LORD is merciful and gracious, slow to anger and abounding in steadfast love.

Psalm 103:8

LET'S PRAY

Thank you, Father, for undeserved favor. Open my eyes to opportunities to extend Your grace to others with my words and actions. In Your gracious name, I pray. Amen.

EMBRACING THE GIFT

What's the most recent evidence of God's favor in your life? Offer a prayer of gratitude for this blessing. Thank Him for the ways family, friends, or strangers have extended grace to you.

SHARING THE GIFT

Consider choosing one of the examples below or follow through on your own ideas for passing along the blessing of grace.

• Speak words of gratitude to store clerks and restaurant servers, even if they make mistakes.

• Withhold unkind responses when someone speaks or acts unkindly.

• Contribute to a stranger's needs by donating food, clothing, and other necessities or volunteer for a ministry your church supports.

• Roll the trash container to the street, or run an errand during inclement weather for an elderly neighbor.

• Share the way God's grace blesses you with someone who may not know Christ or with a fellow believer who needs encouragement.

the gift
of
PLEASURE

There's no table. How can we have a picnic?" I asked my parents. A disappointed ten-year-old, I assumed no table meant no picnic. I'd looked forward to eating lunch beside the river in view of the waterfall.

Mama and Daddy seemed a bit surprised too. Picnic tables were a common sight along this scenic stretch of the river. They got out of the car and walked a short distance to talk while my younger brothers and I watched from the backseat of the '55 Chevy. Surely Daddy wouldn't drive back home.

Mama was a cheerleader for fun, so we didn't want to miss the picnic she'd planned. Despite our limited income, she devised creative ways to entertain us. We once took a ride down a long dirt road where a kind man gave us three pet rabbits. And I still remember the backyard hunt for a buried treasure chest filled with bottles of bubble soap and small toys.

This occasion promised fun by the river, but with no table, I wondered if it would happen.

I saw Mama shrug, and I guessed they'd cancelled the picnic. To my surprise, Daddy opened the trunk and walked to my door carrying the box of food Mama had packed. "Let's go have a picnic," he said.

The three of us scrambled out of the car as fast as rabbits from a cage. Daddy winked at Mama and walked toward the river. He led our family of five to ford the shallow river, one large rock at a time.

Midstream, he stopped on a flat boulder, sparkling with mica in the sunlight. Mama whipped a tablecloth and picnic lunch out of the cardboard box so quickly, we laughed.

Sitting cross-legged on the granite table, we feasted on pigs in a blanket, apple slices, and homemade oatmeal raisin cookies. We watched the water cascade from the falls, flow downstream, and swirl around our rock. What an unforgettable adventure.

My parents reached deep into their hearts and pockets to provide necessities for us, but they went far beyond basics. They wanted to delight us.

Jesus taught a mountainside crowd about how the Father provides for His children. God not only meets our needs, but He also delights our hearts. Jesus posed questions to His listeners. "Which one of you, if his son asks him for bread, will give him a stone? Or if he asks for a fish, will give him a serpent?" (Matthew 7:9-10).

He continued, "If you then, who are evil, know how to give good gifts to your children, how much more will your Father who is in heaven give good things to those who ask him!" (v. 11). God's good gifts include bread and fish, but also times of enjoyment.

God could have created a black and white world for us, but His creation of blue skies and green grass calms and delights us. They remind us of His power. He created us with five senses, including the sense of hearing so that we could enjoy a gurgling stream, a friend's phone call, and the pastor's message.

My parents provided love and fun despite limited resources, but God fills our lives with pleasure out of His inexhaustible love and resources. He created rabbits, waterfalls, and laughter. Family and friendship were His idea. Sunrises and sunsets bookend our days and make us smile.

TABLE TIP

GAME NIGHT WITH SALAD

Invite friends to join you for Game Night and ask each guest to bring a salad to share. Use photo stands, clip photo holders, or an indoor clothesline to display pictures of the people you invite. Provide crackers, drinks, and dessert. After dinner, enjoy the pleasure of each other's company while you play a fun game. Take more photos to record the joyous occasion.

I'm thankful for all God's gifts, including the "extras," like the time our family ate a picnic lunch on the river rock table. And for parents who loved us and taught us to love Him.

If you then, who are evil, know how to give
good gifts to your children,
how much more will your Father who is in heaven
give good things to those who ask him!

Matthew 7:11

LET'S PRAY

Heavenly Father, thank You for meeting my daily needs and
adding extra pleasures. When I watch the hummingbirds or

walk around our neighborhood, I take a deep breath and appreciate Your blessings. Remind me to pause and notice the world You created, the people You placed in my life, and the enjoyment You planned. In Your Son's name, I pray. Amen.

EMBRACING THE GIFT

Place a small notepad on your table. For three days, jot down the sights or moments you enjoy. Will the aroma of muffins baking in the oven or bacon simmering in the pan bring pleasure? Maybe you'll notice flowers you'd never seen before or enjoy conversation with a friend in the grocery store. Perhaps a passage of Scripture will prompt you to praise God and sing a hymn. Thank Him for the gift of pleasure. It was His idea.

SHARING THE GIFT

Look for ways to share joy with someone this week. Could you take breaktime treats for overburdened coworkers or take doughnuts for your Sunday classmates? Maybe you'll draw a picture with a child or laugh with a family member about a funny memory. If you place a devotional book on a park bench, you could share God's truth and the gift of enjoyment with a stranger.

the gift
of
SALVATION

For the first time ever, I interrupted the dinner blessing. My iced tea glass rocked and nearly fell over when I jumped up, sprinted around the table, and grabbed our son, Matt, by the shoulders.

"What did you say? I can't believe it! Did you say what I thought you said?"

He nodded with a grin.

Matt and his sweet wife had joined us for dinner. Normally, Ray prayed, but this time our son volunteered. "Lord, we thank You for the blessing of family and for this food You provided. And we thank You for the blessing of the baby who will join our family."

That's when I interrupted the prayer.

After embracing our son, I hurried to hug the mommy-to-be. Questions about the projected due date and how she felt cascaded like a waterfall. The good news about our expected grandchild brought great joy.

One night long ago a mysterious visitor announced good news about another baby. The angel's unsuspecting audience of shepherds likely rested on bone-hard ground instead of padded chairs like ours.

Unlike the pleasant aroma of our family dinner, the pungent smell of animals encircled the men in the field.

Some of the shepherds guarded the animals while others of those night shift workers snored. Still others may have rubbed aching feet or rolled their eyes at the silly antics of their sheep. Whether the men slept or not, the bright light of God's presence illuminating the pasture startled and terrified them.

An angel's voice broke the silence. "Fear not, for behold, I bring you good news of great joy that will be for all the people. For unto you is born this day in the city of David a Savior, who is Christ the Lord" (Luke 2:10-11).

The angel directed the awestruck men. "And this will be a sign for you: you will find a baby wrapped in swaddling cloths and lying in a manger" (v. 12). After hearing the angel's instructions and praise from the heavenly choir, the shepherds had no trouble deciding what to do next. They hurried toward their Savior in Bethlehem.

The startling proclamation of the long-awaited Messiah's birth interrupted more than the shepherds' rest. It paused world history and changed it forever. The birth of Jesus created a dividing line between centuries of waiting and the fulfillment of Old Testament prophecy of the Messiah. No wonder the heavenly chorus praised God, and the shepherds heeded the angel's words.

The celestial messenger spotlighted a glorious gift—the gospel, the good news of Christ, born to save us from sin. "For by grace you have been saved through faith. And this is not your own doing; it is the gift of God" (Ephesians 2:8).

In response to His gift of salvation, we can confess our sins to God in prayer, accept Jesus's death on the cross as payment for them, and give our lives to Him. We can move toward the Savior as quickly as the shepherds did without delay. We can trust His promise in John 1:12. "But to all who did receive him, who believed in his name, he gave the right to become children of God."

TABLE TIP

DINNER AL FRESCO

Enjoy a meal al fresco, weather permitting. Serve lunch or dinner on the porch, deck, or with sack lunches in the park. Or plan a meal based on foods the shepherds ate in biblical times. You might choose stew, bread, goat cheese, olives, cucumbers, melons, almonds, and dried fruit.

The words of Jesus in John 14:6 assure us He is the way to have an eternal relationship with God—the only way. "I am the way, and the truth, and the life. No one comes to the Father except through me."

Once we become God's children, our generous heavenly Father places another gift on the table—faith to trust Him and embrace the message the shepherds heard: "Fear not." In relationship with Jesus, we can stand against fear instead of yielding to its frightening whispers.

The interrupted blessing at our dining table announced the birth of our first grandchild and filled our hearts with happiness. The blessed interruption of the shepherds' quiet evening issued "good tidings of great joy" which reverberate to all who accept Him as Savior, now and in eternity.

I am the way, and the truth, and the life.
No one comes to the Father except through me.

John 14:6

LET'S PRAY

Dear God, thank You for offering the gift of salvation and adopting me as Your child. Teach me to live in a way that pleases You and shows other people the joy and grace of Jesus in my life. When I struggle with fear, remind me of Your presence and power. In the name of my Savior, I pray. Amen.

EMBRACING THE GIFT

If you've accepted the gift of salvation and given your life to Jesus, have you written your personal testimony? This may seem challenging, but simply write what your life was like before you knew Christ, how you came to know Him, and share the difference He makes in your life. Ask God to lead you to share your story with others. If you have not yet accepted Jesus's gift of salvation, read the verses below and ask Him to reveal Truth to you.

SHARING THE GIFT

Make a list of people in your circle of influence who may not know Christ and pray for them. Memorize verses about salvation so that you'll be prepared to share them. Here are a few: Romans 3:23, Romans 6:23, Romans 5:8, Romans 10:9-10, John 3:16.

the gift
of GOD'S
NOTICE

Twelve-year-old Tyler Marie gripped my hand. "How far above the gorge *are* we? I think the elevator punched holes in the clouds on our way up."

I laughed at her imagination. "Well, we're high enough to have an adventure, that's for sure."

We exited the restaurant tower's glass elevator and followed the host to our table beside the window.

Niagara Falls looked tiny from our lofty view, but our height didn't diminish its majesty. I opened the menu but couldn't resist looking out at the falls. The landscape below us demanded my attention. "It looks like rainbows are falling from heaven and bouncing in the mist over the river."

While we talked and ate, the revolving dining room moved imperceptibly. When the server delivered coffee and cream-topped mousse sprinkled with chocolate shavings, she said, "When I seated you, this table faced west. Now you're facing west again, just in time for the sunset."

Fiery-orange clouds nestling into the horizon captured our attention. Another front row seat to God's creation and majesty.

During dessert, we compared our aerial view of Niagara Falls to what we'd seen earlier that day. We'd stood on the sidewalk near the crest of the American Falls and enjoyed the top-to-bottom perspective. The aquamarine river cascaded over the cusp of the falls and filled our ears with its roar. The sheer volume of the water overwhelmed us.

Earlier that afternoon, we'd purchased tickets and donned slickers and rain hats for a boat ride to the foot of the waterfall. To the tourists in the helicopters circling above, we must have appeared as tiny dolls bobbing in a toy boat atop the waves. "Rain" misted our faces when we looked skyward. Another perspective, beautiful and breathtaking.

We saw the falls from three different perspectives—from the boat, the restaurant above, and the crest of the falls. Ordinarily, our earthbound humanity allows us to see only one perspective—the one right in front of us. Often, this one-dimensional view makes us forget that a heavenly future awaits us. And in the in-between, the abundant, joy-filled life we can experience as Christ walks with us.

God's majestic view of our lives, however, is vastly different from ours.

Psalm 33:13-14 reminds us that our Creator sees every detail. "The LORD looks down from heaven; he sees all the children of man; from where he sits enthroned he looks out on all the inhabitants of the earth."

But He's not a passive observer, watching the events scroll by like so many news reels. He's our heavenly advocate, shepherding the events of our days for our good and His glory. From Genesis to Revelation, the Bible reveals His power and lordship over all the days of our lives.

He numbers and ordains every moment (Psalm 139:13), and He promises to care for us.

Ephesians 2:4-7 describes how He calls us to salvation, grows us in wisdom and Christlikeness, and one day will usher us into the wonders of heaven. "But God, being rich in mercy, because of the great love with which he loved us, even when we were dead in our

TABLE TIP

PEOPLE COUNT

Watch the people you pass along your way this week or see in a restaurant or drive-through line. Notice the number who appear sad, tired, or dejected and the number who look happy and carefree. Speak cheery greetings or words of appreciation to let someone know you noticed.

"We hurt people by being too busy. Too busy to notice their needs.

Too busy to drop that note of comfort or encouragement or assurance of love. Too busy to listen when someone needs to talk. Too busy to care."

—Billy Graham[2]

trespasses, made us alive together with Christ—by grace you have been saved—and raised us up with him and seated us with him in the heavenly places in Christ Jesus, so that in the coming ages he might show the immeasurable riches of his grace in kindness toward us in Christ Jesus."

My family's once-in-a-lifetime views from the bottom, the middle, and the top of Niagara Falls gave us a glimpse of what it's like

2. Billy Graham, Quotefancy, 2023, https://quotefancy.com/billy-graham-quotes, accessed February 15, 2023.

to see beyond what's right in front of us. The Bible describes God's past, present, and future perspective not only on my life, but on all our lives. How can we not trust Him to care for us—yesterday, today, and tomorrow?

The LORD looks down from heaven; he sees all the children of man; from where he sits enthroned he looks out on all the inhabitants of the earth.

Psalm 33:13-14

LET'S PRAY

Gracious heavenly Father, thank You for the gift of Your notice. Your care in the past and in the present assures me my future is secure in Your hands. Remind me to share all my concerns with You, knowing You see, hear, and understand. In the name of Jesus, I pray. Amen.

EMBRACING THE GIFT

Draw three columns and label them Past, Present, and Future. Under the Past and Present headings, list blessings that evidence God's notice and care for you. In the Future column, list your questions and concerns. Ask God, who sees all, to provide and remind you He notices. As you read your Bible, pay attention to evidence He notices and cares.

SHARING THE GIFT

Although our view doesn't compare to God's, He helps us notice other people's needs. Sometimes He leads us to partner with Him in meeting those needs. Give your day to Him and ask Him to help you notice the joys and sorrows of others so you can "rejoice with those who rejoice, weep with those who weep" (Romans 12:15). Look for ways God leads you to minister to others in His name.

the gift of GOD'S HOLY SPIRIT

Erik the Red, my marmalade cat, demanded attention. During my teen years, Erik would often snooze on my bed while I studied at a dropleaf table that served as my desk. Every hour or so, he'd jump down, mosey over to the table, and tap me with his paw.

The name suited my beloved pet whose personality and ruddy appearance resembled the Viking explorer in history books. The curious cat surveyed every inch of our house.

One night, worried about a history test and frustrated by a lost pen and scattered notecards, I left the room to get a glass of water. As I walked down the hall, I glanced back. Erik sprang from the bed to the table and paw-raked pencils and notecards to the floor. Then he yawned, stretched, and curled up atop my textbook. Like the famous Erik the Red, my feline explorer had conquered additional territory.

When I returned with my water, I chided him. His pointed ears twitched as if to say, "Who cares?" I smiled and shook my head. The whiskered drama king simply wanted to be the center of attention. Cats are like that. Once I petted him, his purr engine roared to life.

The short break and rearrangement of my notecards provided more efficient study on my decluttered table. Despite the hilarity of his adventure, my pet's actions taught me a lesson—when fatigue or frustration thwarts progress, swat away distracting thoughts. Rest, re-order, and refresh for improved focus.

Sometimes I need to declutter my mind as well as my desk. Worries, undone tasks, and extraneous ideas cloud my thinking and hinder my progress. They form internal earplugs that muffle God's voice of peace and direction.

The enemy of our souls also befuddles our thinking and distracts us from biblical truth. He pounces onto our shoulders and claws at our minds with accusing hisses and confusing growls.

Despite the enemy's evil schemes, we don't need to be afraid like a mouse trapped between a cat's paws. God provides a powerful gift to renew our minds and teach us—the gift of His Holy Spirit. He lives in the hearts of believers and prays for us (Romans 8:26).

Jesus identifies this member of the Trinity. "But the Helper, the Holy Spirit, whom the Father will send in my name, he will teach you all things and bring to your remembrance all that I have said to you" (John 14:26).

Our Helper infuses our minds with truth and clears out confusion and deceit. Through prayer and Bible study, He enables us to swat away the enemy's lies and curl up to rest in His presence.

As we read the Bible, God's Spirit teaches us about His character and how to trust Him. We read about His faithfulness in the lives of Moses and Paul and learn how we can be faithful. God's care of the Hebrew people during their wilderness wandering demonstrates how He cares for us. He uses Bible passages to convict us of sin and restore our fellowship with the Father.

The Holy Spirit applies the truths of God's unchanging Word to our individual lives. When we study and memorize portions of the Bible, He brings passages to mind when we need them. For example, when someone wrongs us, He may remind us to live "bearing with one another and … forgiving each other" (Colossians 3:13).

TABLE TIP

END TABLE, COFFEE TABLE, OR
BEDSIDE TABLE BASKET

Choose a basket to hold items you use for Bible study. Include pens, a notebook or journal, Bible highlighters, a devotional book, and a 'Thought Capture' notepad to jot down potentially distracting ideas that pop into your mind. Place the basket and your Bible on the table near your favorite reading spot. The basket will remind you to pull up a chair to God's table.

The Spirit's leading never contradicts the written Word. His messages always resonate with Scripture and help us overcome worry, fear, and negative thinking.

Have you ever tried to find something in a desk junk drawer or among papers strewn on a desktop? Frustration sets in, and we lose precious time trying to find a bill or pen. In the same way a cleared physical space aids productivity, an uncluttered mind opens the door for the Holy Spirit's teaching.

I learned a valuable lesson from my mischievous cat who cleared my desk. I'm continuing to learn how God's Spirit teaches and guides me once I purposefully listen. He leads me to rest, reorder, and refresh for improved focus.

*But the Helper, the Holy Spirit, whom the Father will send
in my name, he will teach you all things and bring to your
remembrance all that I have said to you.*

John 14:26

LET'S PRAY

*Heavenly Father, thank You for the gift of Your Holy Spirit.
When my mind fills with doubt, worry, fear, or simply too
many thoughts, give me clarity. Speak to me as I pause to pray
and study Your Word. Convict me of sin and teach me how
to follow You. Amen.*

EMBRACING THE GIFT

Declutter one small space on a desk or counter in your home. Feel
better? Ask God to help you rest, reorder, and refresh your mind, and
fill it with truths from His Word as you read it today.

SHARING THE GIFT

When you study the Bible this week, ask God to teach you more
about relating to other people with His love. Watch for answers in
His Word. Draw a heart and write in it one verse the Holy Spirit
highlights. He clears the clutter and guides us through His Word to
help us share His gifts with others.

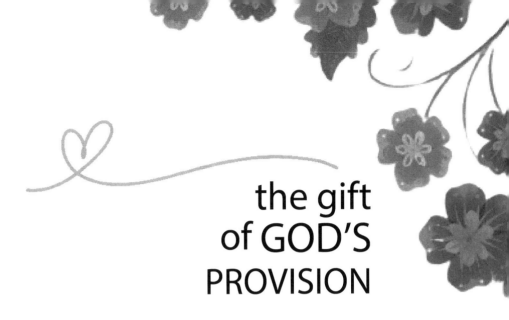

the gift of GOD'S PROVISION

Two weeks after Tyler Marie was born, my friend Cynthia called. "I'd like to see the baby and visit with you Tuesday. If that's okay, I'll bring lunch around noon."

I responded with gratitude. "I'd appreciate that so much. See you Tuesday."

Cynthia arrived, food in hand. "I wanted to bring the tuna salad you like and fruit, but I had to stretch my food budget until payday. God always provides though. I made chicken and dumplings for our dinner tonight from the ingredients I had and thought you'd enjoy some."

"I love chicken and dumplings and appreciate your visit."

God supplied a delicious meal from my friend's sparse pantry and stirred in sweet table conversation as we ate.

We can trust Him for physical necessities and spiritual blessing. Even if our food pantries are full, our *faith pantries* may stand empty at times. My faith pantry needed restocking several decades ago when Ray and I adjusted our budget and bought a larger home.

We realized we'd made a mistake in calculating the monthly house payments when we saw the closing figures. The amount on the bank form presented challenges.

We limited spending and postponed renovations, but I feared the worst and often asked, "What are we going to do?"

My sweet husband reminded me of God's faithfulness and led us in prayer. One day at a time, our heavenly Father restocked our faith pantries as we learned to trust Him. God soon provided Ray with an extra job and helped us figure out how to save money and cover our bills.

Like me, the poor widow who met the prophet Elijah years ago had memories of pantries—both food and faith.

When God sent His prophet to this starving mother, Elijah asked her for water and bread. No doubt the thought of her son's gaunt face and her dread over his impending death gnawed at her heart like the physical hunger in her stomach.

She said, "I have nothing baked, only a handful of flour in a jar and a little oil in a jug. And now I am gathering a couple of sticks that I may go in and prepare it for myself and my son, that we may eat it and die" (1 Kings 17:12).

The heartbroken widow planned to prepare her son's last meal—not his favorite dishes, but a small cake of bread. Destitution robbed her of hope and shrouded her with fear.

Elijah said, "Do not fear; go and do as you have said. But first make me a little cake of it and bring it to me, and afterward make something for yourself and your son. For thus says the LORD, the God of Israel, 'The jar of flour shall not be spent, and the jug of oil shall not be empty, until the day that the LORD sends rain upon the earth'" (vv. 13-14).

The woman may have questioned the prophet's request, but God provided enough in her faith pantry to move her to action. She must have stared, mouth agape when table scarcity turned to plenty. Perhaps she cried tears of relief into flour-dusted hands and yielded to laughter erupting from the depths of her soul. God fulfilled His

TABLE TIP

TURN OVERRIPE BANANAS INTO A QUICK-PREP TREAT

Mash and add overripe bananas to a boxed banana nut bread mix. Add additional chopped pecans or walnuts, cinnamon, and chocolate chips, if no one in the house is allergic. Bake according to directions. Slice when cooled and share with neighbors or co-workers.

promise as Elijah had prophesied. The widow and her son ate not only for one day, but for many.

Jesus's words in Matthew 6:31-32 calm our fears and worries. "Do not be anxious, saying, 'What shall we eat?' or 'What shall we drink?' or 'What shall we wear?' … Your heavenly Father knows that you need them all."

If the poor widow had not experienced need, she might have missed the miraculous gift of God's provision. Need sharpens our awareness of our Provider. In a particular season, we may ask Him for necessary material goods. At other times, we may yearn for more faith, more time to help a neighbor, or more wisdom for tough decisions.

God is Jehovah Jireh, our Provider. We can trust Him and stand against the enemy's lies about what we seem to lack. The God who cared for the desperate widow knows our needs. We don't need to fear.

Cynthia didn't fret when she didn't have enough in her pantry. She provided lunch and conversation with the food and time God gave her. He asks us to do the same—to share the time and material goods He gives us. To be the answer to someone's prayer.

Do not be anxious, saying, 'What shall we eat?' or 'What shall we drink?' or 'What shall we wear?'... Your heavenly Father knows that you need them all.

Matthew 6:31-32

LET'S PRAY

Father, help me to keep my faith pantry always overflowing by trusting Your promise to meet my needs. Help me turn from worry to trust and share Your provisions with others. In Your matchless name, I pray. Amen.

EMBRACING THE GIFT

Write one example of God's provision for each of these categories: home, time, employment, and material goods. Now list three needs to share with God in prayer. Reread our key verses and thank God you can trust Him for current and future needs—even before you see evidence.

SHARING THE GIFT

Take an inventory of your pantry of blessings and plan to share with someone else. What about delivering a freshly baked loaf of bread from your kitchen or a bakery to a neighbor? You might buy extra toiletry items and donate them to a women's shelter along with gently used clothing and purses. Perhaps you could lead your friends in a coat, hat, or glove drive for poor citizens of your community.

the gift
of GOD'S
HOSPITALITY

My friend Glenda placed a lid on her stewpot and muttered, "Não faço ideia porque cozinhei tanto."

Glenda's husband Jimmy heard her Portuguese words and walked into the kitchen. "What are you saying? What's wrong?"

"I said, I have no idea why I cooked so much. Three cups of rice and three pints of black beans. We have Tuesday's leftovers. I don't know why I felt inspired to cook them again."

Jimmy chuckled as he grabbed the car keys and his Bible. "Let's go, Honey. It's time for church. Who knows? Maybe we'll have visitors today. You always like to invite them here for lunch."

After the service, Pastor Will stopped Jimmy and Glenda. "I'd like you to meet the Silva family, Miguel and Camila and their daughter, Sofia. They moved here from Brazil last week." He turned to the visitors. "Glenda grew up in Brazil with missionary parents."

"Bem-vindo à nossa igreja," Glenda said. "Welcome to our church."

Jimmy smiled. "Yes, welcome to our church. Please come join us for lunch. Glenda cooked extra."

Glenda smiled and translated.

On the way to the car, Glenda said to Jimmy. "I should have cleaned up the kitchen. The sink is full of dirty dishes. I'm glad they're coming though. I'll just add a salad to the rice and beans. We do have *plenty*."

Jimmy laughed with his wife. "I wonder if Lydia in the Bible had a sink full of dirty dishes when she invited guests into her home."

In Acts 16, we discover Lydia, like Jimmy and Glenda, chose spontaneous hospitality. Lydia was a businesswoman in Philippi who sold purple cloth. She worshiped God and attended prayer meetings beside the river with other women (13-14).

As they gathered one Sabbath, the apostle Paul and his companions joined the women. Lydia listened as Paul taught, and the truth of Christ in his message changed her heart. At the convenient riverside location, Paul baptized Lydia and her household (v. 15).

With an open heart, Lydia opened her home and insisted Paul and his companions stay there. "If you have judged me to be faithful to the Lord, come to my house and stay" (v. 15). They accepted. I picture Lydia beckoning to them and saying something like, "Come on now. I'll finish the lentil stew I started this morning, and you can tell me more about Jesus." The eager hostess surely showered her guests with hospitality.

Our heavenly Father welcomes believers into relationship with Him. He offers divine hospitality with the warmth of His presence and bountiful provision. He offers rest for our weariness (Matthew 11:28) and comfort for our distress (2 Corinthians 1:3-4). He awakens us each morning with beautiful sunlight and tucks us in at night with the promise of His protection and care.

Fellowship with God equips us to "show hospitality to one another without grumbling." Jesus teaches us to love God and love our neighbor as ourselves (Matthew 22:34-30). The opportunity to open our homes provides one way we can demonstrate our love for God and the people we meet. The joys of hospitality can also help us win spiritual battles against self-centeredness and a complaining spirit. We can share the love of Christ in our homes, no matter the mess.

TABLE TIP

HOSPITALITY MADE SIMPLE

Save easy-prep meal ideas in a computer file or notebook. Gather non-perishable ingredients for each dish and place them in a basket, bin, or large plastic bag on a guest meal shelf in your kitchen. Enjoy sharing hospitality with a smile. Remember, the fellowship is more important than the furniture. Keep it simple.

With the simple and spontaneous response to God's call, Glenda and Jimmy welcomed guests to their table for rest, comfort, and a simple meal. The Silva family enjoyed more than rice and beans that day. They found the heartwarming gift of hospitality wrapped in the love of Jesus and Christian fellowship. I wonder how many opportunities I've missed to provide acceptance and love in our home. I want our guests to sense a heartfelt "You're welcome here" when they cross our threshold.

What's on your table? Be it rice and beans, lentil stew, or donuts, remember Jesus honors a cup of water given in His name (Matthew 10:42). Keep it simple, my friend.

Show hospitality to one another without grumbling.

1 Peter 4:9

LET'S PRAY

Heavenly Father, thank You for the examples of Glenda and Lydia. I want to extend hospitality without grumbling so that I can share Your love with others. May those who gather in my home leave with Your peace and joy. Amen.

EMBRACING THE GIFT

Does your heart need refreshing with the comfort of God's hospitality before you can bless others? He offers gracious reception when we read His Word and talk with Him. Enjoy His presence today and ask Him to help you share hospitality with others. Cultivate the gift and enjoy table times with your guests.

SHARING THE GIFT

How can we manage hospitality at busy times? Adopt this motto: "Advance preparation makes spontaneity possible." Chop extra vegetables for later use, or pop bags of purchased veggies and desserts into the freezer. Double a recipe and freeze leftovers for a meal to share with guests the following week. If your week is too busy for guest meal preparation, remember coffee and pie (even a frozen one) pair well with conversation. Put out a colorful welcome mat and greet your guests with the love of Jesus and a smile.

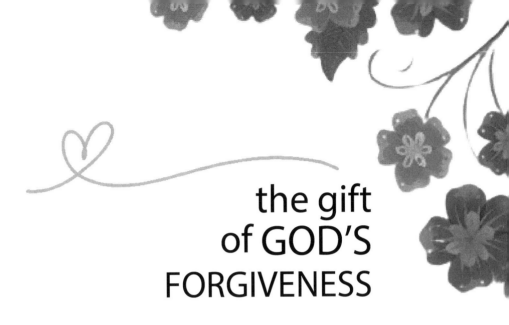

the gift
of GOD'S
FORGIVENESS

Impatience tainted my response when Ray asked, "Are you sure you packed everything into the car? You'd better recheck."

"Yes! I've checked twice. I'm *sure* I have everything."

I kissed him, told him I love him, and traveled 300 miles with my friend Lisa to attend a conference. When we unpacked her Jeep, I realized my garment bag was missing. The bag with most of my clothes. The conference center's remote location offered no shopping options. "I only have enough clothes for half of the sessions," I said.

I called Ray. "We're here, but my garment bag is not. I don't know what to do."

"Don't worry. I'll bring it first thing in the morning."

The next day my knight in shining armor traveled 600 miles round trip. I hugged him and thanked him multiple times.

When I returned home, and we sat at the dinner table, I said, "Please forgive me, Honey, for ignoring your advice to recheck what I'd packed into the car. I was stubborn and impatient. I'm so sorry you had to make that long trip."

The sparkle in his blue eyes preceded his words. "Of course, I forgive you," he said, standing and pulling me into a hug.

I wonder how many times in fifty years of marriage we've said to each other, "I'm sorry. Will you forgive me?" or "Absolutely, I forgive you." We've been far from perfect, but a willingness to forgive and seek forgiveness has nurtured God-given growth into our marriage.

Forgiveness helps every relationship and honors Christ's command—and example. "Be kind to one another, tenderhearted, forgiving one another, as God in Christ forgave you" (Ephesians 4:32).

As far back as the book of Genesis, we see the power and beauty of unconditional forgiveness displayed in the life of Joseph as he endured his brothers' jealousy and evil acts toward him (Genesis 37, 39-50).

Dropped into a pit by his siblings, left to die, and sold to Egypt-bound slave traders, Joseph had every reason to hate his brothers. Enslaved in a foreign land, falsely accused of attempted rape, and abandoned in prison, he had every reason to hate his Egyptian masters.

But Joseph remembered God.

At the appointed time, God lifted Joseph out of prison and exalted him to power in Egypt just in time to save his family from famine. But his brothers didn't trust God or understand forgiveness like Joseph did.

Along with enough grain to feed his starving family in Canaan, Joseph offered his brothers comfort and forgiveness. And he explained the reason he could forgive them. "Do not fear, for am I in the place of God? As for you, you meant evil against me, but God meant it for good to bring it about that many people should be kept alive" (50:19-20).

Joseph foreshadowed Christ. Our Lord forgave the unforgiveable in those who crucified Him. "Father, forgive them, for they know not what they do" (Luke 23:34). And He forgave us when He took on our sins and purchased our salvation on the cross. "It is finished" (John 19:30).

I'm thankful Ray didn't stop loving me even after he drove 600 miles to bring me my clothes. I'm even more grateful God doesn't remove His gift of forgiveness when I sin. As Christians, we're secure in

Jesus. But He still calls us to confess our sins and trust in His forgiveness (1 John 1:9). And to forgive others as He forgives us.

TABLE TIP

A FORGIVENESS TABLE OF MANY COLORS

Plan a meal based on the story of Joseph as a reminder God calls us to forgive as He forgives us. Choose a table runner "of many colors" to represent Joseph's coat and use colorful napkins. You might consider using mismatched dishes and including a colorful fruit or vegetable tray to add to the theme. Add multigrain bread to represent the grain Joseph gave his brothers during a famine when he forgave their ill treatment.

Be kind to one another, tenderhearted, forgiving one another, as God in Christ forgave you.

Ephesians 4:32

LET'S PRAY

Gratitude overwhelms me when I think of Your forgiveness, Father. When I gave my life to Jesus, You welcomed me into Your kingdom and forgave my sins against You forever. When I struggle to forgive, remind me of what You've done for me. Help me to readily forgive like You have forgiven me. Amen.

EMBRACING THE GIFT

Draw two circles. In circle one, write a prayer thanking God for His matchless love and forgiveness of your sins.

In circle two, write any offenses others have done to you. Remember Joseph's attitude. He trusted God with his brothers' sins and forgave before they even asked.

Consider your circles. If we're being honest, the magnitude of God's forgiveness of our sins helps us to forgive others. Pray for anyone who hurt you and forgive as Christ has forgiven you. If you need to ask someone to forgive you, go quickly and seek their forgiveness.

SHARING THE GIFT

When a friend or family member suffers from harboring unforgiveness in their heart, lovingly share how God enables you to forgive, and describe the joy and freedom God offers when we obey. Pray for the offender and ask God to strengthen your friend or relative to forgive.

the gift
of the BIBLE

Three days after I moved into my college dorm room, I discovered a letter in my post office box.

Mama must have a serious message to share. She only uses her yellow rose stationery for important matters.

I rushed to my room, tore open the envelope, and read her words.

Sunday, September 20

My dearest Jeannie,

My thoughts and prayers were filled with you tonight as I attempted to sleep, so I came to the table in your empty room to write to you. I miss you already.

Today you began a new and exciting chapter. I pray with all my heart God will bless your college days and the rest of your life.

I love you with all my heart,

Mama

Decades later, when I reread the treasured greeting in Mama's handwriting, I'm reminded how much she loved me. I reminisce about the table where she sat to reveal her heart to me in a letter. She'd painted that table so I could use it as a high school homework desk. Later, she sat there to write to me.

Mama wrote, reaching out to me from a human, but limited, heart of love. God, in His letter, the Holy Bible, and with love we can't comprehend, reaches out to us. Jeremiah 31:3 says, "I have loved you with an everlasting love; therefore, I have continued my faithfulness to you." He pours out His love for us through His words. Not everyone has memories of a devoted mom, but Romans 8:16-17 tells us everyone who follows Jesus becomes a well-loved, adopted child of the heavenly Father.

God desires for us to read His Word daily as a love·letter from His Father's heart. When we leave it unread on a coffee table or bedside table, we forfeit its value and miss receiving His power for living.

The writer of Hebrews describes the Bible. "For the word of God is living and active" (4:12). The words never change, but God's Spirit meets us individually and applies the truth of the Bible to our hearts to teach us any time we read it. His Word is *His* Word. The final Word. The inerrant, unchanging Word.

The beautiful collection of messages from His heart teaches, changes, and encourages us, and when we read and meditate, God increases our faith and shows us how to honor Him. The more we read, the more we want to read, and our desire to follow God's pattern of life for us increases. We see how He points us to His truth and warns and guides us away from Satan's lies.

God has given us His Word to transform us to the likeness of Christ. Seven months before I received my mother's letter, I discovered the power of God's Word to change my life. Biblical teaching led me to give my life to Jesus and study the Bible with expectancy to know more about God and what He wanted for me. God changed my indifference to a continous thirst for Truth.

CELEBRATING GOD'S LIVING LETTER

The first words the Bible records God speaking are in Genesis 1:3. "Then God said, 'Let there be light'; and there was light." Light a candle or lantern on your table after you clear the dinner dishes. Rest for a few minutes and write a note of encouragement to someone. Check out how the apostle Paul wrote letters that included prayers and encouragement that we read today. Your letter will become a treasured keepsake.

God's faithfulness displayed throughout Scripture bolsters our faith. We learn to trust the One who equipped Moses, protected Daniel, guided Paul, and raised Jesus with resurrection power. His faithfulness assures us we can trust His promise to always accompany us and provide help in troubling times. We can depend on Him because His character does not change. We can trust His words, like those in John 14:27 which soothe our ruffled hearts. "Let not your hearts be troubled, neither let them be afraid."

Bible study also motivates us to relate to others with Christlikeness by responding with love and service as my mom did. We can speak to others with encouragement from God's Word and listen to the wise, biblical counsel of friends.

When we unwrap the gift of God's Word daily and read it as the letter it is from a loving Father to His child, our hearts become tender toward Him, and we respond with awe. The more we learn of His character, the more we understand our need for His instruction and encouragement.

My mother sat at the table in my bedroom and wrote a letter to me. Whenever I open Mama's letter and ponder its precious pages, the deeper into her heart I see. God penned His letter through inspired scribes. Through His Word, He shows us our need for Christ and reveals the beautiful gifts of love from His unlimited supply that rest on His table—provisions for every single need we'll have today and every day. The more we read the Bible, the deeper into His heart we'll see.

For the word of God is living and active.

Hebrews 4:12

LET'S PRAY

Father God, thank You for the priceless gift of Your living Word. Renew my soul as I study and teach me how to honor You with my life. Fill me with Your wisdom and an increased desire to hide Your Word in my heart. In Jesus's name, I pray. Amen.

EMBRACING THE GIFT

Read your Bible, even if for a few minutes, every day. Ask God to use His living letter to teach, encourage, and change you. Memorize and meditate on one verse this week which speaks of His love for you. Which one will it be?

SHARING THE GIFT

Write a letter to someone you love or a trusted friend. Tell them how the Bible affects your life and share encouraging verses with them. Invite them to study a short book of the Bible with you and meet periodically to talk about what you learned. Offer to read the Bible to an elderly person who can't physically attend church. Ask the person what the Bible means to them.

the gift
of HELP
in TRIALS

At age ninety-three, my friend Ramona is losing her sight but not her joy. Age may be weakening her body, but she's one of the strongest women I know because she sees trials differently from most. She talks about the gift of God's help during hard times.

After forty-eight years of marriage, Ramona lost her husband to cancer. Not long after, deteriorating vision forced her to surrender her driver's license.

I shared lunch with her at a local cafeteria one day to find out how she still radiates joy.

"With my macular degeneration, I can't read my Bible, but God is so kind to me. I can listen to sermons or an audio Bible app and play worship music at home, and I always have a ride to church. I listen more carefully than ever to His Word. I miss my sweet husband something terrible. But God's been teaching me He's all I need. I can depend on Him. I know Tommy is in heaven with Jesus, and I'll be there with him one day."

Ramona has prayed for God to remove her macular degeneration like she prayed for God to remove her husband's cancer. But as the apostle Paul learned when he asked God to remove "a thorn" in his side, Ramona has learned, "My grace is sufficient for you, for my power is made perfect in weakness" (2 Corinthians 12:9). I might have responded to God with whining. But Paul responded with the same faith I observe in Ramona's life. "For the sake of Christ, then, I am content with weaknesses, insults, hardships, persecutions, and calamities. For when I am weak, then I am strong" (v. 10).

Paul responded with faith and hope because he knew trials drive us to our sovereign and loving God who promises to help us. While imprisoned in Rome, Paul wrote, "And we know that for those who love God all things work together for good, for those who are called according to his purpose" (Romans 8:28). Paul accepted "all things," even hard times, because he knew God's character and promises. He believed we benefit from all God does and allows. Through difficult times, our Father teaches us truths about who He is that we would learn no other way. He shows us we can depend on Him for help.

Although our understanding of a trial may be as foggy as blurred vision, the study of Scripture helps us clearly see the goodness of God. We don't always notice immediate results of His blessings in troubled times, and we can't understand all His ways, but we can trust God and His promises.

If you're like me, you're not anxious to sign on the dotted line for more challenges and difficulties, but we can trust God and count on His help. Each trial (no matter how severe) has a blessed purpose.

Ramona responds to trials with joy, not because she *sees* all the blessings, but because she *sees* the heart of her Father, knows His character, and hears His voice of encouragement and hope. She reminds us that God sees us, hears our prayers, and offers us His strength— even during the storms of life. Rejoicing in suffering has produced a tremendous harvest of hope in Ramona—and a great sense of humor despite her trials.

At the cafeteria table, I asked Ramona to share her struggles with vision loss. She said, "Well, you know I can't see much with this macular degeneration. One Sunday I went to the downstairs restroom at

TABLE TIP

PUZZLE NIGHT

Invite friends or family to join you for Puzzle Night. After a light meal, place the puzzle pieces on the table and assemble as you visit. You may want to place a card on the table that reads, "Trials are like puzzles to us, but God sees the whole picture and has the answers."

church. While I washed my hands and prepared to leave, two men walked right in. I said, 'Oh my stars! Either y'all came into the wrong restroom or I did.' I dried my hands and rushed out."

Ramona threw back her head and laughed at the memory.

Like Ramona and Paul, we, too, can learn to depend on help from God even in trials. Our loving Father promises to work even our most difficult trials together for our good.

And we know that for those who love God
all things work together for good,
for those who are called according to his purpose.

Romans 8:28

LET'S PRAY

Father, Your gifts are always good, including the gift of Your help in trials. I don't understand all Your ways, but I know You're always kind. When I complain, remind me to thank You in all things and to trust in Your good purposes. Amen.

EMBRACING THE GIFT

When trials come, let's commit to responding like the column on the right and ask God to forgive us and strengthen us when we respond like the column on the left.

RESPONSES TO TRIALS

Complain and harbor bitterness toward God or the people in your life.	Thank God for His faithfulness and your relationship with Him.
Fret and worry.	Read Romans 8:28-29 and trust God's goodness.
Try to determine a solution on your own.	Pray for God's wisdom and guidance.
Focus on your weakness and inability to endure the current ordeal.	Read 2 Corinthians 12:10 and depend on the strength of Christ.
Repeatedly verbalize the inconvenience or pain of the situation.	Look for benefits and trust God's help and purpose when you can't see good in trials.

SHARING THE GIFT

Pray for friends suffering through difficult times and share the passages of Scripture God has used to strengthen you during a difficult time. As Ramona loves to do, help them laugh without trivializing their pain. Or simply make them smile from your kindness toward them.

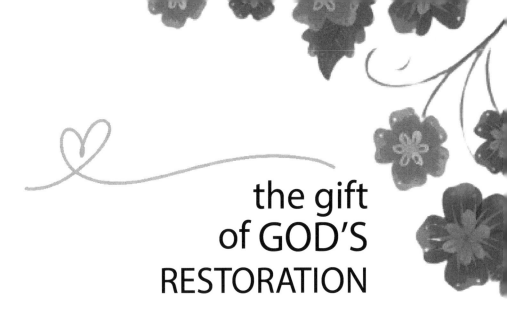

the gift
of GOD'S
RESTORATION

Ray, Tyler Marie, and I joined guests from around the globe to view a collection of world-famous paintings. We meandered through the Impressionists exhibit and then entered the Baroque section where a painting by Rembrandt captured me. *The Denial of St. Peter.* [3]

Tyler Marie leaned over the velvet rope. "It looks like light is shining from the canvas."

With dabs of cream and white oil paint, Rembrandt had created the illusion of light from a girl's candle. The glow exposed the disciple Peter in his darkest moment. The moment of his betrayal of Jesus Christ. Rembrandt's paint strokes etched deep sorrow into Peter's face.

Only hours before, Peter had pledged to Jesus, "Lord, I am ready to go with you both to prison and to death" (Luke 22:33). Jesus responded, "I tell you, Peter, the rooster will not crow this day, until you deny three times that you know me" (v. 34).

But in the poignant moment Rembrandt depicted, Peter denied Jesus when the servant girl accused him of having followed Him. "Woman, I do not know him" (v. 57).

Two more times, Peter denied his Lord.

Then a rooster crowed.

"And the Lord turned and looked at Peter. And Peter remembered the saying of the Lord, how he had said to him, 'Before the rooster crows today, you will deny Me three times.' And he went out and wept bitterly" (vv. 61-62).

While I stood staring at the masterpiece, Ray and Tyler Marie had moved on to view other paintings. I turned to follow but glanced back over my shoulder. I couldn't take my eyes off the painting's dark background. Jesus stood with His hands bound behind His back, surrounded by Roman guards, and gazed at Peter.

My family returned twice to retrieve me, but each time I requested a few more minutes. The anguish in Peter's face and the deep sorrow Rembrandt revealed in our suffering Lord from Luke's passage, pierced my heart.

When my family returned the third time, Ray said, "I think we've devoured enough art for one day. Let's go devour some food in a restaurant."

I glanced back again when we left, and I smiled because I remembered the scene in the painting wasn't the end of Peter's story.

Around the lunch table, we talked about the moment Christ restored Peter back into fellowship with Him.

After Jesus's death and resurrection, Peter had gone for a night of fishing with some of the other disciples. A fruitless night of fishing. From the shore, a man called to them, "'Children, do you have any fish?' They answered him, 'No.' He said to them, 'Cast the net on the right side of the boat, and you will find some.' So they cast it, and now they were not able to haul it in, because of the quantity of fish" (John 21:5-6).

John said to Peter, "It is the Lord!" (v. 7).

That's all Peter needed to hear. He threw Himself into the sea and swam to Jesus, leaving the others to bring in the boat with a net full of fish.

Jesus was preparing breakfast over a charcoal fire. When the fire's aroma filled Peter's nostrils, his mind must have filled with memories

THRIFT STORE TABLESCAPES

Repurpose thrift store finds for informal centerpieces and tablescapes.

Paint old vases, group them in the center of the table, and add flowers or greenery.

Fold a vintage tablecloth to a ten-inch width. Sew down the sides to create a table runner.

Use an old wooden tool caddy to hold napkins, silverware, small pots of ferns or herbs.

Place a potted succulent on top of a stack of vintage books.

Arrange potted plants in a pretty basket or place a jar of flowers in an old teapot.

Paint a bowl-shaped light fixture. Place it on a tray or plate and add fruit, plants, pinecones, or greenery.

of another charcoal fire—the one in the high priest's courtyard where he'd warmed his hands while denying he knew Jesus[4] (John 18:15,18).

Peter had denied Jesus three times. That morning by the fire, Jesus asked Peter if he loved Him three times. In response to Peter's affirmative answers, Jesus commissioned Peter to teach and care for His sheep—for those who'd follow Him. Perhaps Peter recalled the words of Psalm 23:3. "He restores my soul."

Denial over one fire. Restoration over another.

Peter understood both the agonizing pain sin brings and the gift of restoration Christ offers. He became one of the evangelists Christ used to build His church. He preached with boldness about the death and resurrection of Jesus and called for others to repent and follow Him (Acts 2:14-41).

Peter didn't wallow in guilt or allow despair and remorse to rule his life. He embraced God's gift of restoration as readily as the men had accepted grilled fish on the beach.

He did nothing to earn the freedom that accompanies restoration. Like us, he didn't deserve the gift, nor did his actions warrant the blessing. Jesus paid for it on the cross—for Peter, for me, and for you. Once we turn from our sin and turn to Christ, we can throw ourselves into the sea of Christ's restoring power and swim toward His open arms.

He restores my soul.

Psalm 23:3

LET'S PRAY

Dear Father, sometimes sorrow over my sin consumes me. Remind me to turn to You in repentance and accept Your restoration as Peter did. I want to enjoy the refreshing blessing of daily fellowship with You. Thank You for this precious gift. Amen.

EMBRACING THE GIFT

Find a picture of Rembrandt's painting *The Denial of St. Peter* online. Imagine the pain Peter's sin brought and the joy he experienced after he swam to Jesus for restoration. Jesus was waiting for him.

Is there a sin in your life you consider too appalling to even mention? Remember how Peter promised he'd die or go to prison before denying Jesus and then denied knowing Him—three times. Jesus forgave him, restored him to joyous fellowship, and guided the work He'd assigned to Peter. Pray the words of Psalm 139 and accept Christ's restoration. He's waiting for you.

SHARING THE GIFT

Maybe you know a believer who thinks her sin is too appalling for God to forgive. Pray first, and if God leads you to speak with her, you might share the story of Peter's denial, other biblical examples of Christ's forgiveness or your own. He's ready to forgive and restore our fellowship with Him.

the gift of
SELF-CONTROL

Penny's uncharacteristic action startled me. As Ray and I drove to the vacation chalet we'd rented with my brother Carson and sister-in-law Penny, I'd explained my desire to reduce sweets. "I'm always nibbling on something," I said. "Pastries, cookies, and fudge—especially fudge. Sugary fudge chock-full of nuts."

"Like the fudge you bought at the candy store on the way up?" Ray asked, raising one eyebrow. He chuckled and shook his head. "When it comes to fudge, there's no stopping you."

"Well, it wasn't my fault," I said with a chuckle. "The aroma from those swirling pots of chocolate just drifted to the sidewalk and lured me inside. Those confectionary delights taunted me through the glass dividers like cute puppies at the shelter who cry, 'Pick me. Pick me.'"

"Besides, I bought plenty to share." I opened the box and passed it to Penny and Carson in the back seat. "There's chocolate pecan, white chocolate, peanut butter, and even key lime fudge."

At the chalet, Penny and I sipped coffee at the kitchen table. "I don't want to spoil my appetite for dinner," I said. "I'm going to pinch off only a few tiny bites of this chocolate pecan fudge to nibble on."

And nibble I did. Tiny bites. Lots of tiny bites.

After we'd chatted awhile, Penny surprised me. She grabbed the box of fudge, plopped it on the counter, and handed me an apple. I'd known my sister-in-law for forty years, but I'd never seen this side of her. She's gentle and considerate. Not one to take charge.

"What?" I asked, eyebrows raised.

She giggled. "It was an intervention."

"An intervention?"

Penny tilted her head. "Well, you said you planned to avoid excess sweets, so I helped you. Although you didn't help *me* when I devoured those oatmeal cookies from the bakery."

"I'm sorry," I said laughing. We agreed for the rest of the trip to enjoy treats in moderation and remind each other to make wise choices.

Unlike Penny and me, Daniel in the Bible exemplified someone who made wise decisions.

When King Nebuchadnezzar conscripted the prophet Daniel and three of his Hebrew friends into service, Daniel chose to honor God. The king provided the finest foods and wines for the men as part of their three-year indoctrination into Babylonian culture. "But Daniel resolved that he would not defile himself with the king's food, or with the wine that he drank" (Daniel 1:8).

Daniel was far from his native country. No one at home would have known what he ate, but he resolved to honor God instead of embracing all the king's extravagancies. Maybe the palace foods weren't on the Jewish kosher list, but whatever the reason, Daniel chose to honor his convictions and please God instead of succumbing to temptations. His decisions required courage, determination, and discipline.

Like Daniel's, our determination, empowered by God, enables us to obey and honor Him by controlling our actions. Self-effort lasts only a short while and won't make us holy. Only God's power can strengthen us to refrain from sinful attitudes and actions and obey His commands day by day. Because the Holy Spirit indwells, teaches, and empowers us, we can choose self-control like Daniel did (Philippians 2:13). God produces this fruit that reflects Jesus in our lives.

TABLE TIP

WORDS FOR THE WISE

If you want to remember this quote, print it on a card, and place it in a clip photo holder on your table.

"Sow a thought and you reap an action; sow an act and you reap a habit; sow a habit and you reap a character; sow a character and you reap a destiny."

—Ralph Waldo Emerson[3]

Although we will always struggle with sin, the Holy Spirit helps us resist temptation and exercise discipline to flee from sin and run toward His commands. As believers, we have daily opportunities to honor God with our decisions. His power fills in the gap of our weaknesses and enables us to live for Him one godly choice at a time.

We can encourage the resolve of fellow believers to choose self-control like Penny did for me, but only the Holy Spirit can grow this God-honoring characteristic in our lives.

But the fruit of the Spirit is love, joy, peace,
patience, kindness, goodness,
faithfulness, gentleness, self-control.

Galatians 5:22-23

---

3. Ralph Waldo Emerson, Goodreads, Inc. 2023, https://www.goodreads.com/quotes/416934-sow-a-thought-and-you-reap-an-action-sow-an, accessed February 20, 2023.

LET'S PRAY

Father, draw me closer to You and help me, through the power of the Holy Spirit, to choose self-control. Enable me to honor You with my attitudes and actions. In the name of Jesus, I pray. Amen.

EMBRACING THE GIFT

When you're tempted to overindulge in areas like food, drink, spending, or entertainment, ask yourself, "Do I truly need this? Will my choice honor God?"

Read Hebrews 4:16. "Let us then with confidence draw near to the throne of grace, that we may receive mercy and find grace to help in time of need." Ask God for the power to resist. For accountability, share your struggle with a trusted friend who will encourage you.

SHARING THE GIFT

Self-control in your life could bless and encourage others.
• If we refrain from overspending, we can give more to our church, a ministry or people in need.
• If we choose a healthy lifestyle, we'll have more energy to serve God and others.
• If we spend less time on entertainment, we can be present for the people in our lives.

Imagine your peace and the blessings others will enjoy when you make God-honoring choices and embrace the gift of self-control.

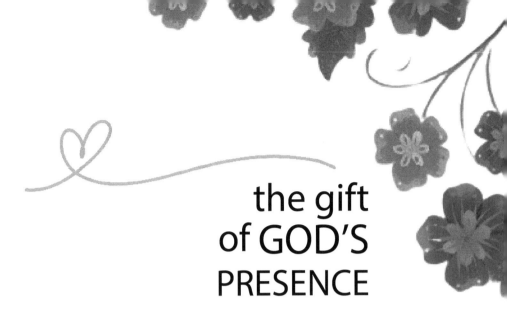

the gift of GOD'S PRESENCE

Ray and I turned off the television, silenced our phones, and gathered the family around the dining room table. We leaned forward, mesmerized as my father-in-law, Red, shared story after story about his World War II Army service. Tyler Marie, then a teenager, videotaped Red's account. We wanted not only to hear, but to remember his every word.

"Before the war, I worked at the shipyard in Savannah all day and played minor league baseball at night, living the good life. Until the day I opened the notice to report for duty.

"At boot camp in Florida, a sergeant discovered I was the best map reader in the barracks. My skill surely helped when we landed in the Pacific and had to navigate those islands with basic maps."

Our son, Matt, peered over Red's shoulder to look at the map we'd spread out on the table. "Where were you, Grandpa?"

Red pointed to a tiny island. "At first, we were right about here in a small village. We had no idea what we'd face. Sometimes when the sergeant moved our squad to a new location, we'd have no shelter or food rations for a day or two while we waited for the supply trucks. We dug holes to sleep in at night."

He stared off into the distance for a moment. "And, man, were we scared. Any combat veteran who says he wasn't scared is lying. Bullets flying past your head and bombs exploding nearby. One night the sky lit up, and I saw trees and buildings blown to bits. The impact was louder than thunder and vibrated the ground. We only survived by God's help."

Red gave us more than a history lesson. He enthralled us with stories we'd never heard before about the war. He commanded our full attention. Nothing else mattered.

When Jesus visited the home Mary shared with her brother, Lazarus, and sister, Martha, nothing but listening to Jesus mattered to Mary. He captured her attention. She sat at His feet, mesmerized by His teaching. Martha, however, dashed around the house fretting and fuming as she prepared a meal (Luke 10:38-40).

Martha complained to Jesus. "Lord, do you not care that my sister has left me to serve alone? Tell her then to help me" (v. 40).

Imagine the tone of her words. I picture her sighing, pushing up her tunic sleeves, and scowling at her sister, who appeared oblivious to Martha's labors.

Instead of reprimanding Mary's choice, Jesus affirmed it. "Martha, Martha, you are anxious and troubled about many things, but one thing is necessary. Mary has chosen the good portion, which will not be taken away from her" (vv. 41-42). Surely, Mary treasured His words for the rest of her life.

Jesus didn't condemn Martha for bustling about preparing food. Instead, he pointed out her anxiety and misplaced priorities. Martha's busyness hindered her from hearing the words of Jesus designed to penetrate and change her heart. Mary cherished His presence and His words. She valued Him more than any other person or task.

When we have the opportunity to spend time with Jesus, are we a Mary or a Martha?

Before the crucifixion and resurrection, believers had access to Christ only when He physically visited with them. Christians now

TABLE TIP

A PORTABLE TABLE

Take flowers from your yard, pretty napkins, and a simple meal to share with a lonely person. Prepare a dish or pick up a pizza. Set the table and invite God's presence when you pray before the meal. Be a good listener while the dear one you visit enjoys the gift of your presence. During the conversation, ask about favorite foods and plan the next visit.

have access to Jesus every moment of our lives. He's always with us. His Spirit indwells us. If we could only understand how amazing this truth is. And how real the gift of Christ's presence is. He's Immanuel, "God with us" (Matthew 1:23).

When busyness causes us to scramble from one daily chore or pleasure to another, we forfeit the joy of His company. We miss the intimacy of His presence and often the guidance He offers— and we need.

Jesus invites us to turn our hearts and attention to Him, Mary-style. She sat at His feet and listened to Him. We can sit at His feet and "listen" to Him through His Word.

Picture Mary's face turned upward, soaking in every word Jesus spoke. Surely, she mirrored the joy she saw in His. The author of Psalm 16 described this truth. "In your presence there is fullness of joy" (v. 11).

If you want to experience the same fullness of joy Mary experienced, pick up your Bible and sit in the presence of Jesus today and every day.

Mary, who sat at the Lord's feet and listened to his teaching ... has chosen the good portion, which will not be taken away from her.

Luke 10:39-42

LET'S PRAY

Thank You, Father, for Mary's example. Each day, help me prioritize spending time with You, enjoying Your presence. I want to know You like Mary did and honor You in all I do. In the name of Jesus, Immanuel, I pray. Amen.

EMBRACING THE GIFT

Jesus extends a daily come-as-you-are invitation. An opportunity to rest, talk, listen, and learn. A time to thank and praise Him. A time to sit at His feet and get to know Him better through the pages of the Bible. List your daily priorities in order of importance and ask God to help you to choose wisely.

SHARING THE GIFT

Who could you devote undivided attention to this week? Make it a priority to take a walk or share a cup of coffee with them. Share something you've learned from your time sitting at the feet of Jesus and enjoying His presence.

the gift
of GOD'S
COMPASSION

My friend Dawn and I watched Steve, a Christian in our community, leave his meal on a table near us in a local café. He walked outside and approached a skinny, disheveled man with stringy hair, hole-filled tennis shoes, and a dirty jacket pulled up to his ears.

Dawn fretted over Steve's abandoned meal. "His food's getting cold, and it's cold outside. What's he doing out there?"

Steve leaned over and extended a hand to the skinny man who crouched down on the sidewalk, arms wrapped around his body. All smiles, Steve nodded and spoke with him.

Soon the pair entered the restaurant together and pulled out chairs at Steve's table. The man whispered to Steve who walked to the counter and ordered two ham sandwiches, fries, and a large coffee.

The two men chatted like friends while they ate. As Steve wrote on a napkin, we overheard him explain the directions to a homeless shelter nearby where hot food and a bed softer than the sidewalk awaited.

We finished our lunch and left. In the car, Dawn and I chatted about Steve's compassion. He not only purchased food and coffee for the homeless man, but he invited him to his table—like King David did when he invited a crippled man to eat at his table long ago.

Mephibosheth's heart probably pounded when he received the king's summons to the palace. His father, Jonathan, had been a closer-than-a-brother friend of David's, but His grandfather, King Saul, had tried to kill David. More than once. Would the king kill him?

Mephibosheth bowed before the king. Perhaps David caught a glimpse of his friend Jonathan in his son's eyes. He said, "Do not fear, for I will show you kindness for the sake of your father Jonathan, and I will restore to you all the land of Saul your father, and you shall eat at my table always" (2 Samuel 9:7).

Normally in those days, only relatives and close associates of the king ate at his table. King David could've ordered servants to deliver royal takeout meals to his friend's son. Instead, filled with compassion, he extended an invitation to his table of fine dining.

Much like the homeless man Steve helped, Mephibosheth had nothing to offer with no way to gain favor or repay his benefactor. Lame and fatherless, he entered the king's palace with empty pockets. He left with a full purse—acceptance by the king and a royal meal ticket.

The King of kings invites us to His table, and we come as empty-handed as the homeless man. We cannot earn or repay Him for the riches He provides. They are free gifts from His heart of compassion. Psalm 103:13-14 paints a tender picture of His love for and understanding of His children. "As a father shows compassion to his children, so the LORD shows compassion to those who fear him. For he knows our frame; he remembers that we are dust." Doubt of His loving care disappears when we focus on His compassionate heart.

Jesus modeled compassion when He walked on the earth. He loved and blessed the children His disciples attempted to shoo away (Mark 10:13-16). He healed the sick (Matthew 14:14) and wept with Mary in grief over the death of her brother, Lazarus (John 11:32-35). Luke records the way Jesus responded to a widow whose only son died. "He had compassion on her and said to her, 'Do not weep'" (7:13).

TABLE TIP

SERVE THE SERVER WITH COMPASSION

Share God's compassion with restaurant servers and address them by name. Even if the service is poor, we can be kind. We don't know the problems they may be facing. Ask how you could pray for them and leave a generous tip as God leads you.

The Bible tells us to show compassion to the poor, strangers, and to widows and orphans. Jesus models interactions with despised and ostracized people like the lepers, prostitutes, and tax collectors He met.

New Testament passages urge Christians to minister with hearts of compassion. One example is Colossians 3:12: "Put on then, as God's chosen ones, holy and beloved, compassionate hearts, kindness, humility, meekness, and patience."

That day on the restaurant sidewalk, one homeless man experienced God's compassion when he met Steve. When we have opportunity, God calls us to minister to others.

Put on then, as God's chosen ones, holy and beloved, compassionate hearts, kindness, humility, meekness, and patience.

Colossians 3:12

LET'S PRAY

Heavenly Father, I'm grateful for Your heart of compassion toward me. Open my eyes to those around me who need compassionate words and deeds so, ultimately, they see You. Amen.

EMBRACING THE GIFT

Which example of Jesus's compassion touches your heart the most? Think of two times God has shown compassion to you and write a prayer of thanksgiving.

SHARING THE GIFT

Read Luke 14:12-14 where Jesus teaches us to care for those who can't reciprocate. You may not know a physically lame person, but could you help someone crippled by doubt, poverty, loneliness, or a language barrier? Consider gifting someone with a cup of coffee, a needed pair of socks, or warm conversation. Try smiling at a person learning English and encourage their efforts. You might assist them in finding an English language class in your community.

the gift
of GOD'S
PROTECTION

Gigi, I'm under the table," Mary Claire would call. "Come make a tent and get under here with me."

Our then four-year-old granddaughter scurried to her favorite refuge each time she visited us.

Smiling, I'd grab blankets to drape over the dining room table. Then I'd bend my tall frame and crawl into our house (or palace), whichever Mary Claire designated.

She'd dart in and out to collect stuffed animals and her tea set. She'd hug Poppy, her grandpa, and slip back into the tent. If she'd planned a birthday party for one of the animals, we'd sing and serve pretend cake and ice cream to the honoree, usually a stuffed bear or rabbit.

Our shy Mary Claire liked her table tent hiding place. She found it cozy and secure, out of the sight of other family members or a neighbor who'd pop in. She didn't enjoy it alone though. She preferred my presence. When claps of thunder from an approaching storm frightened her, she'd call for reinforcement. "Poppy, come into the tent with us."

A storm also frightened Jesus's disciples. From a boat on the Sea of Galilee, He'd been teaching crowds of followers on the shore (Mark

4:1-2). When evening came, He instructed the disciples to row to the other side of the sea. As they strained at the oars, Jesus, fully man and fully God, weary from hours of teaching, slept in the boat. When the fierce wind blew water into the boat and it began to fill, they woke Jesus and cried out, "Teacher, do you not care that we are perishing?" (v. 38).

Jesus spoke first to the wind and the waves, "Peace! Be still!" (v. 39). Then He spoke to the disciples. "Why are you so afraid? Have you still no faith?" (v. 40). After they saw the forceful wind and turbulent waves of the sea obey the Lord, they said, "Who then is this, that even the wind and the sea obey him?" (v. 41).

God spoke words to create the seas, and on that stormy day, the trembling disciples watched the sea calm at the sound of the words Jesus spoke. With His presence and His power, we are safe. He promises to defeat our fears as surely as He did for the disciples. The Bible, His Word, assures us of His protection. We can say with the psalmist, "You are my hiding place and my shield; I hope in your word" (Psalm 119:114).

In addition to physical storms, new situations or financial uncertainty can provoke fear. Squalls of tense relationships or work situations can lead us to panic, and a health diagnosis could wash us overboard into a sea of anxiety. Except for God. He's our "refuge and strength, a very present help in trouble" (Psalm 46:1).

Facing storms as we look to our heavenly Father, He strengthens our faith muscles and teaches us to trust Him. He never promised to protect us *from* every storm of life, but He promises to guide us *through* them. He stays closer than two grandparents huddled under the dining room table and offers more comforting words than we ever could. Jesus said, "I will never leave you nor forsake you" (Hebrews 13:5).

Like the disciples, we sometimes attribute more power to life's looming storms than to God. Although Jesus rebuked the disciples' lack of trust, He lovingly guided them and guides us to recognize His

TABLE TIP

NACHOS YOUR WAY

Protect family or friend time by creating a meal together with cell phones silenced. Create a Nachos-Your-Way buffet. Brown ground beef with onions and stir in taco seasoning. Prepare an array of toppings like cheese, salsa, olives, black beans, sour cream, avocado, and chopped tomatoes. Spread tortilla chips on a pan and sprinkle grated cheese on the top. Heat until the cheese melts. Fill your plates and enjoy the fellowship.

presence and learn more of His character. We can depend on His care and His Word to guard our lives.

Life's storms are real, not imaginary like our under-the-table play, and life's trials aren't fun like a stuffed bear's birthday party. Still, when we look toward Jesus, who is in the boat with us, we can trust Him. Our stories of His faithfulness during storms, along with verses we hold to, will encourage others to place their faith in Him.

You are my hiding place and my shield; I hope in your word.

Psalm 119:114

LET'S PRAY

Father, for the storms I'm facing now and for future ones, remind me of Your presence, and teach me through Your Word to trust You more. You are my refuge and strength, a very present help in trouble. I praise Your holy name. Amen.

EMBRACING THE GIFT

Psalm 5:11 says, "Let all who take refuge in you rejoice; let them ever sing for joy, and spread your protection over them, that those who love your name may exult in you." Draw a tent in the margin and add a cross to represent the presence of Christ. Draw a face inside the tent to represent you. Above the drawing, list the storms threatening your peace. Then write Psalm 56:3. "When I am afraid, I put my trust in you."

SHARING THE GIFT

Tab a section in your journal to record examples of God's protection. Include personal stories and those you read in the Bible. As you study, add verses about God's faithfulness. When friends face trials, pray first, and share a story from your list or a favorite verse to encourage them.

the gift
of GOD'S
KINDNESS

That's too much trouble, Margaret," I said to a dear friend, "but what a kind idea. The hospital room is too small. There's not even a table."

"It's no trouble. Your mom was so disappointed when Dr. Jones admitted her. You know how she'd planned to serve dessert to our group of friends at her house. So, we're going to take dessert to her. What's her favorite?"

"That's easy," I said. "Strawberry shortcake."

"Strawberry shortcake it is then. With whipped cream. We'll see you Friday."

"That's really too much trouble in a hospital room."

Margaret smiled. "But it's her favorite, and we're happy to do it. It'll make her day. See you Friday about 3:00."

Despite my argument, the determined party planner invited mutual friends to visit Mama in the hospital. They greeted her with hugs and assembled plates of whipped cream-topped strawberry shortcake on the windowsill shelf.

Margaret pushed the narrow, rolling hospital table over the bed and served my mom. She added a flowered napkin and created a table that rivaled a fancy tea party. Propped on her pillow, Mama chatted with her guests and enjoyed the sweet treat.

While we ate, Margaret elbowed me gently and nodded toward Mama. We saw tears of joy fill her brown eyes. I thought of a verse I'd learned as a young child in Sunday school. "Be kind to one another" (Ephesians 4:32).

Kindness had triumphed over inconvenience in the small hospital room. Margaret and strawberry shortcake co-starred in a show of kindness—in an unlikely place.

In a New Testament account of Jesus sharing kindness, He stopped on the roadside to acknowledge Zacchaeus, the despised tax collector who perched in a sycamore tree to catch a glimpse of the Messiah. Jesus noticed the man clinging to a tree limb. "Zacchaeus, hurry and come down, for I must stay at your house today" (Luke 19:5).

Jewish citizens, frequently cheated by tax collectors, expressed shock that Jesus associated with someone they deemed despicable. And yet, because of the Lord's kindness and compassion, the heart of the ostracized man changed and said, "Behold, Lord, the half of my goods I give to the poor. And if I have defrauded anyone of anything, I restore it fourfold" (v. 8).

Jesus could have retreated for rest, enjoyed fellowship with His friends, or preached to the masses that day. Instead, He extended kindness to one man.

In the same way Jesus changed the heart of Zacchaeus, He changes our hearts when we confess our sins, agree to change our ways, and surrender to His will. "God's kindness is meant to lead you to repentance" (Romans 2:4). With this gift of unlimited kindness, God offers us a personal relationship with Him for our lifetime on earth and for eternity in heaven.

Each morning we can ask God to help us see people through His eyes—like He saw Zacchaeus. We can respond with acts of kindness as elaborate as a dinner party or as simple as a smile, a phone call, or strawberry shortcake. When we extend kindness to others, we focus

TABLE TIP

A BASKET OF CHEER AND KINDNESS

Pack a basket or bag for a rehab, hospital, or nursing facility patient. You might include a notepad and pen for recording doctors' instructions, soft facial tissues, unscented lip balm or lotion, a cheery card or tiny flower arrangement to decorate the bedside table, and a magazine, puzzle book, or devotional. Enjoy a short and cheerful visit.

on their needs and prevent the enemy of self-centeredness from capturing our thoughts.

We can proclaim God's ultimate kindness by sharing our personal testimony and the gospel. The kindness of Jesus changed the heart of a ruthless tax collector, and He changes hearts today when we embrace the gift of His kindness and share it with others.

God's kindness is meant to lead you to repentance.

Romans 2:4

LET'S PRAY

Heavenly Father, thank You for the kindness You extend to me every day. You offer mercy and grace I don't deserve, and

You scatter blessings along my daily path. Open my eyes to someone who needs acknowledgement and encouragement today or a kind word or deed. Help me notice and see people the way Jesus saw Zacchaeus. Lead me to share with others the way Your lovingkindness changes my life. In the name of Jesus, I pray. Amen.

EMBRACING THE GIFT

Think about the words or acts of kindness a friend, family member, or even a stranger has shared with you. How do you feel when someone goes out of their way to acknowledge you or walk the extra mile just for you?

List the ways you've seen God's kindness in His Word and in your life. Then, if you can, take a short walk today. As you go, thank God for His kindness in sending Christ and for the way He shows kindness to you each day.

SHARING THE GIFT

Inventory the talents, gifts, or possessions you could use to show kindness to others. Ask God to lead you to people who need this gift. Do you know someone suffering from a chronic illness or recovering from surgery? She may need a visit or assistance with a challenging task. Would a lunch invitation bless a coworker, or does a friend need to hear about the lovingkindness of Jesus? Consider ways to help others through participation in a church ministry. Note on your calendar a time you plan to share God's kindness and thank Him for opportunities.

the gift
of
PURPOSE

After Mama died, family members selected furniture, jewelry, and other mementos of our beloved mom and grandmother to take home. Children and grandchildren chose books, chairs, framed art, and kitchenware with sentimental value, and we shared family photos. But no one wanted Chestine, the drop leaf table I'd named for her chestnut wood.

Although Chestine had helped us for decades, she stood forlorn and unwanted in the corner of the dining room. The little orphan's top and legs bore scars from years of wear, but I decided to adopt her.

Her longevity, sturdy design, and faithful years of service impressed me. Her purposes had changed, depending on the time or occasion, but she'd served our family well. Thoughts of her varied uses sparked fond family memories.

I remember when the little table stood by a window at my grandmother's house and held a large ceramic lamp. As a child, I loved curling up in the overstuffed chair beside the table to visit with Mamie, my grandmother, or page through issues of *Scenic South*, a southern landscape magazine. Sometimes I could smell a hint of Chestine's perfume—lemon furniture polish.

Years later the table lived in my mom's home against the wall under a large, framed mirror. Most of the time she held a fruit bowl and Mama's mail. When the entire family gathered for meals, however, Chestine proudly wore the title "dessert table." She showcased rich offerings of caramel cakes, pecan pies, and plates of oatmeal cookies. We loved this service she performed.

Now the little table stands in my writing office under a window. Most of the time, with her leaves down, she serves as a decorative piece with a plant and a basket on top. When I raise her leaves, her purpose shifts to that of a personal assistant who holds notebooks and papers.

As I considered Chestine's roles in our family's history and the purposes she's served, I pondered the purposes God designs for believers for His kingdom's work.

God ordains that some will preach from pulpits, and some will show mercy to hurting hearts. Others teach Bible lessons or encourage friends toward godly living. Some, like Ray, are gifted to offer practical help. Others organize events or manage finances to honor God.

God purposed and called Peter to preach powerful messages and Dorcas to tailor clothing. Part of Martha's life purpose was to prepare meals for guests. Lydia extended hospitality to fellow Christians, and Barnabas encouraged Paul. They all worked with their God-given gifts, fulfilling His intended purpose.

Our heavenly Father leads us to places where people need friendship, encouragement, or physical necessities. He planned the ways we'd work alongside Him. The apostle Paul declared to the Ephesians, "For we are his workmanship, created in Christ Jesus for good works, which God prepared beforehand, that we should walk in them" (2:10).

Prayer and Bible study, coupled with the Holy Spirit's leadership and wise counsel, will guide us to our divine purposes.

Like Chestine, who supported lamps in some seasons and displayed beautiful desserts in others, we may use our gifts in different ways as we surrender to God's purpose and work within our life's

TABLE TIP

A BIRTHDAY APPRECIATION MEAL

Have fun creating a centerpiece to honor a friend or family member at a birthday meal. You might include a framed photo, objects to represent their interests or hobbies, and a vase of flowers or greenery. Print small cards with these words. "I appreciate the way you, _____." Before the meal, ask each guest to write on a card a way the guest of honor met a need in their life. For example, "I appreciate the way you . . . encouraged me, helped me, shared generously with me, or offered comforting words." Place the cards in a box, wrap the box with birthday paper, and present it to the honoree.

seasons and responsibilities. Satisfaction and joy fill our hearts when we serve Him well.

As we desire to use the gifts God gives us, He'll provide occasions for us to strengthen or encourage others as we honor Him.

Who knew a little drop leaf table could also be such a fabulous teacher?

For we are his workmanship, created
in Christ Jesus for good works,
which God prepared beforehand,
that we should walk in them.

Ephesians 2:10

LET'S PRAY

Father, thank You for designing me with a purpose—and this purpose is to glorify You as I serve others. Please show me how to use the gifts You've given to me to minister in Your name. Convict me when I'm self-focused, Lord, and direct my attention to people and the needs around me. I want to honor You and fulfill Your purpose for my life. In Jesus's name, I pray. Amen.

EMBRACING THE GIFT

When my granddaughter was four, I could have made cookies much faster if I'd worked alone, but I enjoyed her company, the delightful time we shared, and the opportunity to teach her. God doesn't need help to accomplish His work, but as a loving Father, He calls us to be part of it. When we join Him, we fulfill His plan for us. Ask Him to reveal or confirm His purpose in the joyful, productive life He designed for you. Consider how your gifts, skills, and resources might help the people whose needs attract your attention and touch your heart.

SHARING THE GIFT

Watch for opportunities to do the good works God has planned for you today. What role will you fulfill? Maybe you'll pray with someone who grieves. A new neighbor may need help with a chore, or a church member may need to be included in conversation. Perhaps you sense God wanting you to use your gift of teaching or organization. How will you honor Him to fulfill His (and your) purpose today?

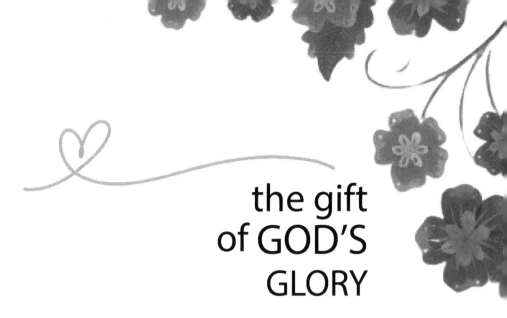

the gift
of GOD'S
GLORY

Juggling my coffee mug, Bible, and journal, I exited the back door to sit in my favorite place to pray and read God's Word. After three days of rain, sunshine beckoned me to my deck table for time with God.

I sipped my coffee and glanced upward to enjoy the clouds and trees against the blue canopy of the sky. The view usually reminds me of God's glorious majesty and presence and fills my heart with worship. This time, however, only brown and white fabric flowers greeted me. My table umbrella with its earth-toned floral pattern obscured my view.

The umbrella may have protected me from sunburn, but it hindered me from soaking in the full beauty of God's creation. The same happened when Jesus came to earth in the form of man.

The prophet Isaiah foretold that when Christ came, nothing about His appearance would draw us to Him (Isaiah 53:2). From the manger to the cross, God would obscure the human eye from seeing the full majesty of Christ by veiling His glory in flesh.

Jesus displayed aspects of His glory when He spoke, healed the sick, raised the dead, and gave His life on the cross. His actions allowed a glimpse into His full character and majesty, the essence of His being—but only a glimpse.

"And the Word became flesh and dwelt among us, and we beheld His glory, the glory as of the only begotten of the Father, full of grace and truth" (John 1:14 NKJV).

Even a limited view of Jesus's glory was enough to amaze believers and lead them to worship Him. Studying God's Word leads me to worship Christ—as does a broader view of God's creation from my deck. I shifted my coffee and Bible to where I could see the treetops stretch toward heaven and watch the clouds parade across the sky.

Like Jesus's veiled glory, I still couldn't see all the trees or every cloud in the sky, even without the umbrella blocking my view. The Milky Way stretches above me in the heavens, but I can't see it all. I dream of gazing at the Northern Lights, but they don't shine for us in Georgia. All the glory of God we see in creation is only a partial view. But one day, we'll see it all. The glory of the Lord will outshine even the brightest lights. "For the earth will be filled with the knowledge of the glory of the Lord, as the waters cover the sea" (Habakkuk 2:14 NKJV).

One day the glory of Christ Jesus, in all His majesty, will shine with more brilliance than the Northern Lights. His awe-inspiring nature will sparkle brighter than millions of multi-faceted diamonds.

Our humanity and our sinful world prevent us from seeing His full glory now, but we can rejoice over what He reveals through creation and His Word. When we read about the parting of the Red Sea and Christ's Resurrection or gaze at a mountain range or a sunset, we can delight in God's greatness.

We may only see a prelude of His glory now—like my partial view of the sky and trees from under my deck umbrella—but what we see can captivate us. Think about the smile of a child. A bud transforming into a fragrant blossom. The crash of ocean waves thundering onto the shore. A roaring waterfall. Consider the stars. God scattered one septillion stars throughout the universe. [5] One septillion is written with

TABLE TIP

NATURE-THEMED TABLESCAPE

Is today a time to refresh with a leisurely walk? Observe glimpses of God's glory in the world He created. Collect rock samples or take close-up photos of moss, ferns, berries, bird nests, or wildflowers. Create a nature-themed tablescape with a burlap table runner and natural decorations. Lay a grapevine wreath on the table. Place jars filled with stems of flower buds or leaves in the center of the wreath. Tie a sprig of rosemary onto linen napkins with twine.

twenty-four zeros, but God knows the name of each star—and He knows our names.

The more glimpses we see into who He is, the more our heads should bow in humble gratitude. As we discover more about the gift of God's majesty and glory, our trust in and love for Him should expand.

When the day comes to see Christ face-to-face in heaven, our glimpses will turn into eternal gazes, and we'll worship Christ our Lord, the One "who is and who was and who is to come" (Revelation 1:4 NKJV).

And the Word became flesh and dwelt among us, and we beheld His glory, the glory as of the only begotten of the Father, full of grace and truth.
John 1:14 NKJV

the gift of GOD'S GLORY

LET'S PRAY

Father, the glimpses of Your glory I see amaze me and make me want to know more about You. Open my eyes as I study Your Word. Create in me an even deeper longing for the magnificence of Your full glory I'll see in heaven. Amen.

EMBRACING THE GIFT

When you read your Bible this week, ask God to teach you more about Him. List any of His attributes you see in Scripture and any reflections of His glory you notice in the world around you. Praise Him for them.

SHARING THE GIFT

Study Matthew 5:16. Commit this week to reflect some of Christ's attributes to those around you. Do you need to ask someone to forgive you? Ask God to lead you to someone you can pour out Christ's love, mercy, or grace onto.

the gift
of a SURE
and ETERNAL
FUTURE

Tyler Marie ran to our car in the parking lot outside her apartment and chattered without taking a breath. It had only been one day since Brad proposed to her, and ideas flowed like whitewater rapids.

"Mom, the botanical gardens would be the perfect place to get married, don't you think? The chapel is beautiful, and there's a big dance floor in the conservatory. Dad, I'll check on the prices. Won't succulents and white flowers be gorgeous for my bouquet? Do y'all need something to drink? Lemonade?"

Ray's eyes widened at Tyler Marie's enthusiasm, but I smiled. "I think the botanical gardens would be lovely. Check the prices, and we'll talk."

During lunch, we mostly nodded as she continued.

"I know the perfect baker for the cake, Mom. And I decided on aqua for the bridesmaids' dresses, but I'll let them pick the style."

After lunch, we wrapped our daughter in hugs and sent her off to plan the wedding of her dreams. "Love you bunches, my sweet girl. Tell Brad we'll see you both soon."

When Ray and I returned to the car, he shook his head. "She's decided *all* those details in less than twenty-four hours?"

"Honey, Tyler Marie has been planning her wedding since she was a little girl. She simply needed to fall in love." With a chuckle, Ray started the car.

Fifteen months later, our baby girl's wedding day arrived.

After the ceremony, with joyful tears still in my eyes, I grabbed Ray's hand and dashed with him ahead of the guests, down the garden path to the conservatory. We swung open the doors and gazed at a glorious sight.

Silver and white decorations sparkled under the lights. Tropical plants flanked the dance floor, and white flowers encircled the four-tier, buttercream-frosted cake. The aroma of beef medallions and fresh-baked bread swirled around the dining tables adorned with potted ferns.

Mesmerizing beauty.

Perfect as planned.

When the music began on cue, we welcomed our guests to the grandest celebration our family had ever hosted.

Conversation buzzed among the guests, but at the master of ceremonies' signal, the room quieted. We fixed our eyes on the door and blinked back tears as we waited for our precious daughter to enter with her groom for the long-anticipated celebration dinner—their first step into the glorious future we'd hoped and prayed for.

One day, in the glorious future God has planned since eternity past, Christ and His Bride will enjoy an even grander wedding celebration in a far more magnificent location (Revelation 19:7). At the appointed time of Christ's return, a symphony of instruments will join a chorus of voices and fill the air with majestic praise. Plans perfected before time began assure the marriage supper of the Lamb will surpass all others.

We will celebrate the culmination of all God's plans to bring those He loves into eternal fellowship with Him. I can only imagine the joy and unconditional love that will radiate from our Savior's face as He extends His nail-scarred hands toward us—His beloved bride, the church—and welcomes us to His table.

TABLE TIP

FUTURE BLESSINGS

If you're privileged to plan a pre-wedding celebration or help a family prepare for a wedding, you could make a 'Blessing Box' as a gift. First, ask the couple if they would like to have one. Paint a small wooden box and attach a painted wooden letter to represent the couple's last name. Place the box on a table at a shower, a party, or at the wedding reception. Scatter blank cards around it and ask guests to write a prayer, verse, or words of advice related to the bride and groom's future. Present the box of cards to the couple and invite them to read the encouraging words on their first anniversary.

Dressed in sparkling white without a trace of earthly stain, we'll join our Groom. Christ will lavish us with gifts of a pure heart and a heavenly home with jeweled walls and golden streets (Revelation 21:18-21).

I wonder if we'll bow in worship first, burst into songs of praise, or be struck with silent awe. Maybe we'll dance with joy because without Jesus's sacrifice to cover our sin, we would've been denied entrance into this glorious celebration.

"Blessed are those who are invited to the marriage supper of the Lamb" (Revelation 19:9).

Cherished memories of our daughter's wedding celebration still bring smiles, but at ten o'clock that night, the festivities ended. The music stopped. The new couple and the guests drove away. And, as Ray and I walked to our car, the venue manager turned out the lights.

The party was over.

In heaven, the celebration will never end. This gift is sure and eternal. The Bride will join the angels with glorious songs of praise for her Groom, the King of kings and Lord of lords. Joy will reverberate throughout heaven's halls forever and ever, and His Light will never go out.

Will you be there?

With eternal and unconditional love, Almighty God,
the Alpha and Omega, Creator of heaven and earth,
invites the bride of Christ, the church, to
The Marriage Supper of the Lamb
DATE AND TIME TO BE REVEALED
Required for admittance: Salvation
Believe in the Lord Jesus, and you will be saved.
Acts 16:31
Enter into the joy of your master.
Matthew 25:23
Blessed are those who are invited
to the marriage supper of the Lamb.
Revelation 19:9

LET'S PRAY

Dear God, thank You for sending Jesus to die on the cross so that we, Your bride, could join the heavenly celebration of Your marvelous, grace-filled plan. For those who don't yet know You, open their eyes to their need for Your forgiveness and salvation. The Bible says now is the accepted time. In Your matchless name, I pray. Amen.

EMBRACING THE GIFT

We've visited many tables and occasions in these forty devotions. Each one had a purpose, a place in time, and selected people. Picnics are seasonal, parties come and go, but this final table is eternal and only for those who have accepted the invitation.

God's Word is your invitation to a personal relationship with Him and a place at the marriage supper of the Lamb. If you haven't come to Jesus and asked forgiveness for your sins and given your life to Him, don't wait. No one knows when Christ will return. The apostle Paul quoted Isaiah 49:8 in 2 Corinthians 6:2. "Behold, now is the favorable time; behold, now is the day of salvation."

My heart for you is that you have accepted the invitation of Jesus, and one day, we'll be seated together for the grandest celebration of all. If you belong to Christ already, praise Him that you are His, and He is yours forever. Thank Him for His glorious gift of a sure and eternal future with Him, your Bridegroom.

SHARING THE GIFT

Put a place card at each family member's or visitor's plate at the dinner table. Tell them the card marks their reserved place and your love for them. Remind them their birth or adoption or friendship gives them the privilege of joining your family at every meal. Then explain how a relationship with Jesus assures us of a place at His daily table and at the marriage supper of the Lamb.

Surely goodness and mercy shall
follow me all the days of my life,
and I shall dwell in the house of the LORD forever.

Psalm 23:6

ONE MORE
HEARTFELT MESSAGE FOR YOU

Dear Reader Friend,

You honored me by purchasing and reading this devotional. I hope you found platefuls of blessings. If you haven't yet believed in Jesus and surrendered your life to Him, know that life with Him is an amazing journey.

If you enjoyed *A Place at His Table*, I'd be grateful if you'd write a brief review on the bookseller's website to share your thoughts with other readers.

Ponder the truths of Scripture we've read together, and remember, dear one, you don't have to allow fear, worry, and their evil pals to bully you into despair. Continue to read the Bible daily and memorize this truth for believers. "He who is in you is greater than he who is in the world" (1 John 4:4).

Pull up a chair to the place our Father set for you at His table and discover His daily gifts to satisfy your heart.

With the joy of Christ our Lord,

—Jeannie

ABOUT THE AUTHOR

Embrace encouragement from God's Word and share it," is Jeannie's motto. A classic extrovert, meeting people is her favorite hobby. She's the chatty one in shopping lines and waiting rooms who loves hearing the stories others share. With the gifts of gab and encouragement, Jeannie makes friends through writing and face-to-face conversations.

An award-winning writer, Jeannie contributed to two devotionals (Worthy Inspired), five compilations (Lighthouse Bible Studies), and *Focus on the Family* magazine. She writes for *Refresh Bible Study Magazine* and *Hope-Full Living*.

Readers view Jeannie's writing like a warm hug. Her author voice sparkles with encouragement as she shares stories from her southern roots and connects them to biblical truth.

Jeannie combines her love for God and people with treasured table memories in *A Place at His Table*, designed to help readers embrace God's daily blessings. "Instead of allowing fear, doubt, and worry to sabotage your day, pull up a chair to God's table, and find His gifts to satisfy your heart."

Jeannie enjoyed her roles as a classroom teacher, an instructional coach, and an assistant professor. Continuing her passion for teaching, she leads an online English Club-Bible Study for women who are learning English. She is an active member of her church and a mentor for Word Weavers International.

Jeannie is a wife, mom, and Gigi who loves creating family memories, sharing lunch with friends, and cheering for the Georgia Bulldogs. She enjoys picnics, quaint cafés, mountain streams, just-for-fun hikes, vanilla lattes, and historical novels. A converted night owl, mornings find her on the deck sipping coffee, reading her Bible, and enjoying prayer time with God.

Visit Jeannie at JeannieWaters.com where she shares her love for Jesus and ideas for "Connecting with God and Each Other." Find her on social media @jeanniewaters44.

CONTINUING TO EMBRACE GOD'S GIFTS

Jeannie's favorite hobby is meeting people. She'd love to hear from you. Send her an email at Jeannie@JeannieWaters.com or visit her website, JeannieWaters.com, for a free resource. Read uplifting blog posts on the topic "Connecting with God and Each Other."

Jeannie suggests you sketch a simple table at the top of a daily journal page for a few weeks, to remind you of God's blessings. Each morning, praise God and ask Him to meet your needs. Each evening, list the blessings He provided and thank Him. Did you see the beauty of a sunset or find comfort in His Word? Maybe you found an extra serving of needed patience or courage today. Search the pages of your Bible daily for God's blessings and ways to honor Him.

CONTINUING TO SHARE GOD'S GIFTS

If you found blessings in *A Place at His Table,* share the stories and biblical truths with someone dear to you. Surprise friends or relatives with this devotional as a gift. Include a personal note inside the book.

Invite neighbors or members of your small group or book club to read the devotions and study the Scriptures together. Create a surprise table decoration to symbolize the content of the devotions you plan to discuss. You might use a bowl of strawberries for the devotion on Kindness or a picnic basket for Surprises. Have fun making bookmarks with sturdy paper and write a key verse from a devotion on them. Use markers, colored pencils, or stamps to decorate the back.

At a bridal shower, you may choose to read "The Gift of God's Abundance" about designing the wedding cake. Present a copy of *A*

Place at His Table to the bride and the mothers of the bride and groom. It would also make a wonderful hostess, housewarming, birthday, or holiday gift.

You may enjoy sharing a copy with a rehab or nursing facility patient, or perhaps with someone receiving long-term medical treatments.

Enjoy a brief weekly phone call with an out-of-state friend to talk about a devotion.

ACKNOWLEDGMENTS

To my Lord and Savior, Jesus Christ, thank You for loving me and for guiding me to this work. You drew me closer and taught me to trust You more as You led me through these pages. All glory and honor belong to You.

To my dear husband, family, friends, and colleagues who prayed, coached, and loved me to the finish line, I offer heartfelt gratitude. Although invisible to the reader, I see your fingerprints on every page and feel them in my heart. You are among God's greatest gifts.

George and Karen Porter, Rhonda Rhea, and the phenomenal staff of Bold Vision Books, with expertise and enthusiasm, you embraced my ideas based on lessons God taught me and crafted them into a real book. I'm amazed and honored.

Larry J. Leech II, your excellent editing work polished my words to a shiny finish. Amber Weigand-Buckley, your cover design created a beautiful home for my stories and thoughts. Wendy Leech, your design created a beautiful home for my words.

My precious Word Weavers Page 33 critique group, Monketeer friends, Lisa, Elizabeth, Lori, Julie, and Jean, your icing-on-the-cake friendship, writing experience, and reminders to trust God through multiple daily texts both encouraged me and made me laugh.

Marilyn, Beebe, and Katy, your love for God and me gleamed through every email and conversation as you shared faithful prayers, keen observations, excellent questions, and biblical wisdom, always pointing me to Christ.

Edie Melson, you and the late Lucinda Secrest McDowell were the first professionals who believed my idea and my writing were book-worthy. My heart still smiles at memories of those conversations.

My enthusiastic local Word Weavers chapter friends, your invaluable critiques and writing partnership made me a better writer and turned second Sunday afternoons into celebrations.

Jeanie, Linda, and Glenda, your faithful words, prayers, and eagle-eye proofing added shine to my work.

Karen Sargent, you're the best book cheerleader I know. You and Rhonda Rhea tie for the cheeriest email composer prize.

Dear friends in our Sunday morning Journey class, I love studying God's Word with you and appreciate your interest and prayers. Iron sharpens iron.

Dear blog subscribers, your comments on my posts brighten my days and urge me to keep writing. Prayer team members, I appreciate your faithful support. Gene and Karen, our dear friends, you prayed and encouraged me when I doubted.

And dearest of our blessings, our treasured children and grandchildren, your love and support fill this Gigi's heart with joy. Poppy and I are so proud of you, and we're grateful you're ours.

To all of you,
Grace to you and peace from God our Father
and the Lord Jesus Christ.
I thank my God in all my remembrance of you."

Philippians 1:2-3

NOTES

1. "Are You Getting Enough Sleep," National Center for Chronic Disease Prevention and Health Promotion, Division of Population Health, U.S. Department of Health and Human Services, 2022, https://www.cdc.gov/sleep/features/getting-enough-sleep.html, accessed November 4, 2022.

2. "Stress Relief from Laughter? It's No Joke," Mayo Clinic, Mayo Foundation for Medical Education and Research, 2023, https://www.mayoclinic.org/healthy-lifestyle/stress-management/in-depth/stress-relief/art-20044456, accessed January 21, 2023.

3. Rembrandt van Rijn, *The Denial of St. Peter*, 1660, oil on canvas, 154.5 × 169.5 cm, Rijksmuseum, Amsterdam, https://www.rijksmuseum.nl/en/collection/SK-A-3137, accessed December 12, 2022.

4. Jason Soroski, "Why Does Jesus Ask Peter 'Do You Love Me'?" Bible Study Tools, Salem Media Group, December 22, 2022, https://www.biblestudytools.com/bible-study/topical-studies/why-does-jesus-ask-peter-do-you-love-me.html, accessed February 12, 2023.

5. "Stars," NASA Science Universe Exploration, Astrophysics Communications, NASA's Goddard Space Flight Center and NASA's Jet Propulsion Laboratory, NASA's Science Mission Directorate, December 8, 2022, https://universe.nasa.gov/stars/basics/, accessed December 15, 2022.